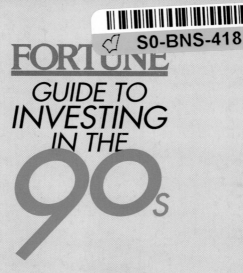

FORTUNE
GUIDE TO
INVESTING
IN THE
90s

Contents

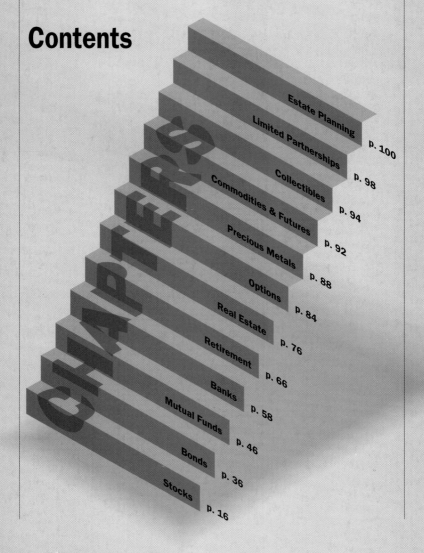

What Size Investment Are You Interested In?

> *Wealth is not his that has it, but his that enjoys it.*
>
> **Benjamin Franklin**

Private Bankers	p. 15
Money Managers	p. 15
Options/Futures	p. 84
Precious Metals	p. 88
Limited Partnerships	p. 98
Portfolio of Stocks	p. 16
Portfolio of Bonds	p. 36
GNMAs, SLMAs, & FNMAs	p. 37
T-Bills	p. 43
T-Bonds	p. 38
Mutual Funds	p. 46
IRAs	p. 66
Bank Accounts	p. 58
EE Savings Bonds	p. 104
Piggy Banks	p. 1

$1,000,000
$500,000
$100,000
$10,000
$1,000
$250
$50

How Much Risk Are You Willing to Take?

FURTHERMORE

Three Faces of Risk

When evaluating an investment, one of the first questions people ask is "How risky is it?" Yet investments that seem low-risk may be deceiving. That's because most of us consider only a single type of risk—**investment risk**—the chance that an investment may lose value. But other types of risk are also important. **Credit risk**, important to bond-holders, is the possibility that a bond issuer may not pay the interest it owes. **Inflation risk** is the chance that a long-term asset's value may not grow enough to keep up with inflation's erosive effect.

High risk in one area may be counterbalanced by low risk in another. For example, stocks have a relatively high investment risk, but a low inflation risk, making them a surprisingly safe investment (in terms of inflation) over the long term. On the other hand, savings accounts, which have a minimal investment risk, have a high inflation risk, making them far less attractive than many of us believe.

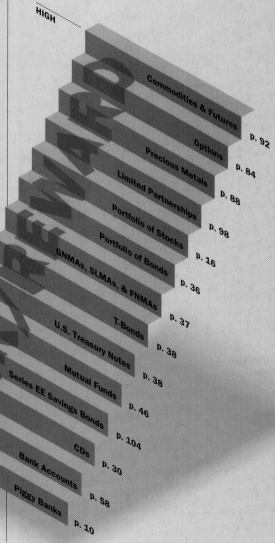

HIGH

RISK/REWARD

LOW

Commodities & Futures	p. 92
Options	p. 84
Precious Metals	p. 88
Limited Partnerships	p. 98
Portfolio of Stocks	p. 16
Portfolio of Bonds	p. 36
GNMAs, SLMAs, & FNMAs	p. 37
T-Bonds	p. 38
U.S. Treasury Notes	p. 38
Mutual Funds	p. 46
Series EE Savings Bonds	p. 104
CDs	p. 30
Bank Accounts	p. 58
Piggy Banks	p. 10

3

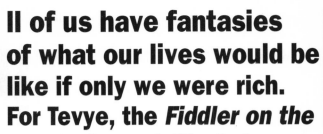

All of us have fantasies of what our lives would be like if only we were rich. For Tevye, the *Fiddler on the Roof* of Broadway immortality, being rich meant indoor plumbing, a yard full of livestock, and numerous requests for advice. Times have changed since the turn of the century—even in Russia—and being rich today has very different connotations. But they are just as personal. ● Most likely, you talk to someone about having—or not having—money every week, if not every day. What does "rich" mean to you? Paying all the bills each month and still having something left over? Getting all your kids through college without taking out a second mortgage? Having enough money saved to quit your job and sail around the world? Everyone has a dream—and a truth—to discover. Where are you now? Where do you want to go? How will you get there? ● A mere 30 years ago, most people thought success was earning $15,000 a year. At that time, a person who could accumulate $250,000 and bank it could live very comfortably on the interest and not have to work. Thirty years of inflation later, someone who earns just $15,000 a year could be eligible for food stamps. That $250,000 barely covers the cost of a family-sized apartment in some urban areas. Time surely changes everything, from one's standards to the value of money.

The Roaring Eighties changed us, too. While the media fawned on the economy's high rollers, it also taught the rest of us what really big money can buy. Anyone with a television set is no longer unfamiliar with hedonism. In a sense, cultural democracy in action now means we all know what kind of wood paneling we'd want in our yacht.

The title of this book is "The Fortune Guide to Investing in the '90s." This is not just investing—an art as well as a science, to be sure—but a pursuit anyone with time, energy, and a modicum of brains can figure out. It's the personal part that's tough. Here is where our needs, feelings, philosophies, desires, even morals converge to play a role of which we may be only partly aware. We take good care of ourselves, or perhaps we don't. We know what we need—the struggle to provide food, clothing, shelter, health care, and education is a given—but do we know what we want? And, just as important, do we know what it will cost?

This book is not about getting rich. Mostly, it is about accumulating the tools you need to take control of your financial life, ask the best questions, and make use of what you find out. This is not a how-to book; it's an empowering, what-is book. If you use it to get rich, all the better.

FURTHERMORE

What Does "Wealthy" Mean to You?

When we started writing this book, we polled more than 100 acquaintances and friends about what they thought **financial** security meant to them. The question: Assuming that you already own your home, how much money would you need in the bank, free and clear, after taxes, to feel comfortable? Not super-rich, but wealthy enough to have all the things you need?

The answers were surprising, not in their wide range (from $50,000 to $10.5 million) but in their uniformity. Roughly 90% of the people we questioned, all of whom were successfully employed in white-collar fields, said they would be happy with $1 million, in cash, after taxes. Certainly, this is a difficult number for most of us. If you earned $100,000 a year after taxes and managed to save $5,000, it would take you 200 years to accumulate a million-dollar pile (not counting investment growth, interest, or inflation). Assuming that your 20 highest earning years are ages 35–55, you'd need to stash away $50,000 each year for your million (again assuming no interest).

But in another sense, $1 million is surprisingly small. If you invested it conservatively and lived off the interest, after taxes you'd have less than $50,000 a year, at 1993 interest rates. Not exactly champagne-in-the-back-of-the-limo money.

This **fantasy** makes an important point. Most of us hope to retire one of these days, and that will require an enormous amount of money to provide sufficient income every year. If you want $50,000 a year on top of your Social Security and pension checks, you'd better start figuring out how you're going to squirrel away your million.

Terms of Enrichment

super-rich	rolling in dough	made of money	flush	well-off
stinking rich	leisure class	money to burn	fortunate	prosperous
filthy rich	opulent	in the money	affluent	solvent
rich as Croesus	deluxe	loaded	well-lined pockets	comfortable
billionaire	millionaire	independent	well-to-do	well-fixed
jet set	wealthy	moneyed	well-heeled	advantaged

GETTING STARTED

When people around you start talking about money, do your eyes glaze over? When you start reading information from your bank, your broker, or even the newspaper, do you start wondering whether your brain cells are malfunctioning? ● Take heart: The problem is not you. Most writing about money is virtually incomprehensible. It's not English, as you and I speak it, but a synapse-stifling combination of awkward prose, inarticulate babble, and insider slang. Just as therapists have their psycho-babble, and New Agers have their crystalspeak, the money world has its own jargon—and feels little compunction to translate it for the rest of us.

WHAT IT SAYS

"Registered Representative"
"Account Executive"
"Financial Advisor"
"Financial Planner"
"Brokerage Vice President"
mean
Stockbroker

WHAT IT MEANS

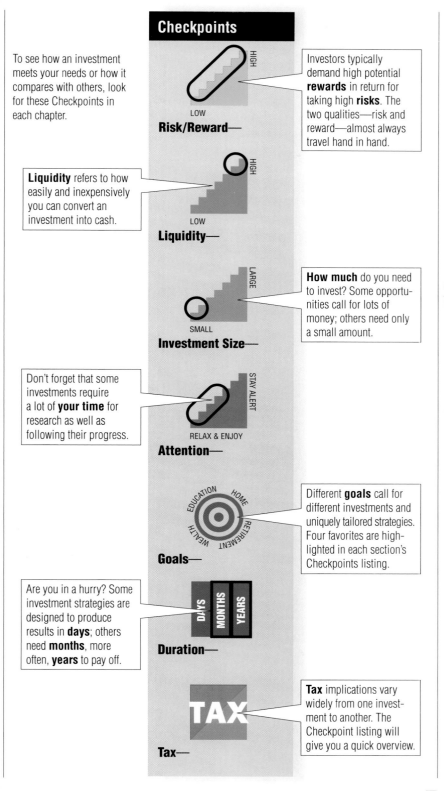

Checkpoints

To see how an investment meets your needs or how it compares with others, look for these Checkpoints in each chapter.

Risk/Reward—

Investors typically demand high potential **rewards** in return for taking high **risks**. The two qualities—risk and reward—almost always travel hand in hand.

Liquidity refers to how easily and inexpensively you can convert an investment into cash.

Liquidity—

Investment Size—

How much do you need to invest? Some opportunities call for lots of money; others need only a small amount.

Don't forget that some investments require a lot of **your time** for research as well as following their progress.

Attention—

Goals—

Different **goals** call for different investments and uniquely tailored strategies. Four favorites are highlighted in each section's Checkpoints listing.

Are you in a hurry? Some investment strategies are designed to produce results in **days**; others need **months**, more often, **years** to pay off.

Duration—

Tax—

Tax implications vary widely from one investment to another. The Checkpoint listing will give you a quick overview.

Living Off Your Savings

Are You a Saver, an Owner, a Lender— or a Debtor?

Your money can work 4 ways: as savings, as loans, as ownership— better known as equity—or as debt, also called leverage. You are probably involved in all 4 areas.

Savings offer liquidity and security, plus a small amount of income.
- Savings accounts
- Money-market funds
- Certificates of deposit

Loans, in the form of "fixed income" investments, provide somewhat less liquidity and security in return for additional income.
- Corporate bonds
- Municipal bonds
- Government securities
- Bond mutual funds

Equity affords still less security and only modest income—but offers a major plus: the chance for substantial appreciation.
- Common stocks
- Preferred stocks
- Stock mutual funds
- Real estate
- Precious metals
- Collectibles

Debt offers the chance to greatly expand the equity you control, but demands regular interest payments and swells your risk of loss.
- Credit cards
- Mortgages
- Home equity loans
- Margin debt
- Short sales

THE NUMBERS

Average Savings of a Household

America's savings rate—a prime indicator of both a family's and a nation's underlying economic stability and resources—is the lowest among the industrial nations. In less than a generation, it has fallen from a solid 9% to less than 3%.

Japan	$45,118	Finland	$12,387
Switzerland	$19,971	Sweden	$10,943
Denmark	$18,405	Ireland	$7,478
France	$17,649	United Kingdom	$7,451
Germany	$17,042	Canada	$6,531
Austria	$16,369	Greece	$4,780
Norway	$15,196	United States	$4,201
Belgium	$15,111		

Source: *Where We Stand*

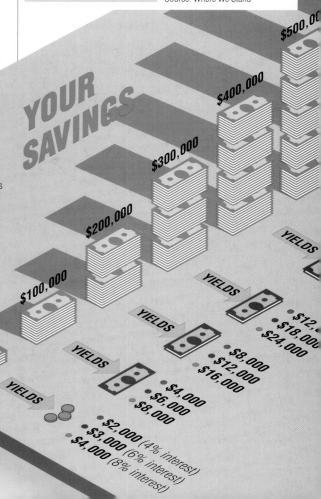

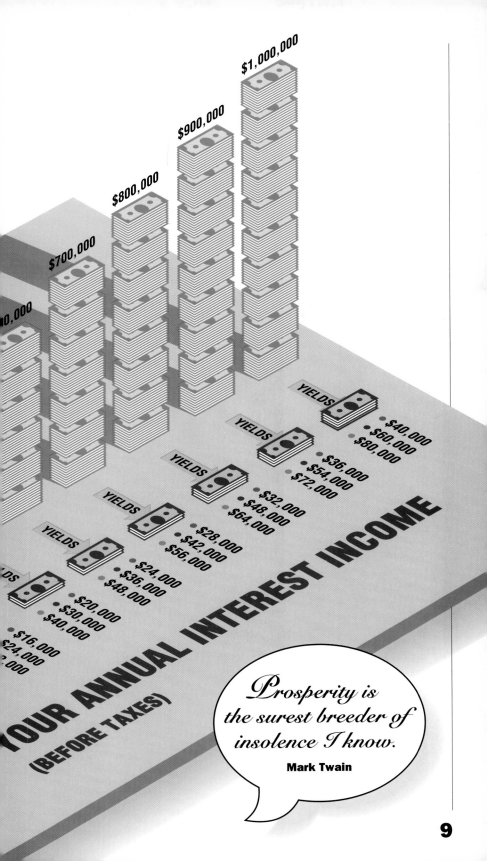

$1,000,000

$900,000

$800,000

$700,000

$0,000

YIELDS • $40,000
• $60,000
• $80,000

YIELDS • $36,000
• $54,000
• $72,000

YIELDS • $32,000
• $48,000
• $64,000

YIELDS • $28,000
• $42,000
• $56,000

YIELDS • $24,000
• $36,000
• $48,000

YIELDS • $20,000
• $30,000
• $40,000

• $16,000
24,000
,000

YOUR ANNUAL INTEREST INCOME

(BEFORE TAXES)

Prosperity is the surest breeder of insolence I know.

Mark Twain

9

How Much Do You Have to Invest?

> *It isn't enough for you to love money—it's also necessary that money should love you.*
>
> **Baron de Rothschild**

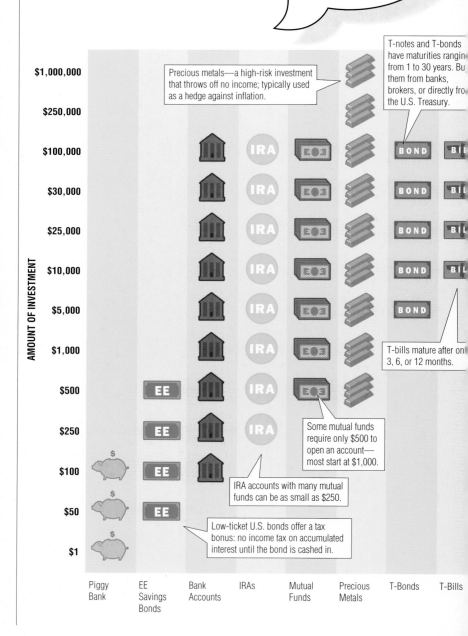

AMOUNT OF INVESTMENT

Precious metals—a high-risk investment that throws off no income; typically used as a hedge against inflation.

T-notes and T-bonds have maturities rangin from 1 to 30 years. Bu them from banks, brokers, or directly fro the U.S. Treasury.

T-bills mature after on 3, 6, or 12 months.

Some mutual funds require only $500 to open an account—most start at $1,000.

IRA accounts with many mutual funds can be as small as $250.

Low-ticket U.S. bonds offer a tax bonus: no income tax on accumulated interest until the bond is cashed in.

| $1,000,000 |
| $250,000 |
| $100,000 |
| $30,000 |
| $25,000 |
| $10,000 |
| $5,000 |
| $1,000 |
| $500 |
| $250 |
| $100 |
| $50 |
| $1 |

Piggy Bank | EE Savings Bonds | Bank Accounts | IRAs | Mutual Funds | Precious Metals | T-Bonds | T-Bills

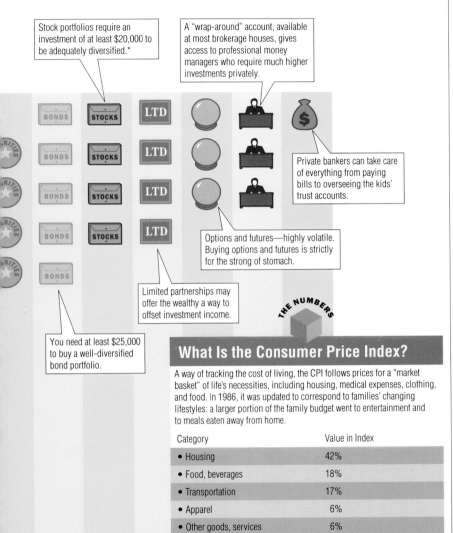

Stock portfolios require an investment of at least $20,000 to be adequately diversified.*

A "wrap-around" account, available at most brokerage houses, gives access to professional money managers who require much higher investments privately.

Private bankers can take care of everything from paying bills to overseeing the kids' trust accounts.

Options and futures—highly volatile. Buying options and futures is strictly for the strong of stomach.

Limited partnerships may offer the wealthy a way to offset investment income.

You need at least $25,000 to buy a well-diversified bond portfolio.

THE NUMBERS

What Is the Consumer Price Index?

A way of tracking the cost of living, the CPI follows prices for a "market basket" of life's necessities, including housing, medical expenses, clothing, and food. In 1986, it was updated to correspond to families' changing lifestyles: a larger portion of the family budget went to entertainment and to meals eaten away from home.

Category	Value in Index
• Housing	42%
• Food, beverages	18%
• Transportation	17%
• Apparel	6%
• Other goods, services	6%
• Entertainment	5%
• Medical Care	5%

Note: Numbers have been rounded off, so they don't add up to exactly 100%.

ie Mae   Portfolio   Portfolio   Limited   Options/   Money   Private
e Mae   of Bonds   of Stocks   Partner-   Futures   Managers   Bankers
ie Mae   ships

*Source: American Association of Individual Investors

Watching Your Money Grow

Switzerland, Japan, and the United States pay the highest worker wages. In Switzerland, the average income for a skilled factory worker is $40,000. In Japan, it's $35,700, and in the U.S., it's $32,000.

Source: *Where We Stand*
Based on 1991 study

Value in 5 years	**$7,973**
Value in 10 years	**$20,926**
Value in 30 years	**$229,916**

THE NUMBERS

How to Save a Million Dollars*

If you stashed money in your mattress each month, here's how long it would take for you to put aside a million bucks.

Saved each month	Number of Years
$100 a month	834 years
$500 a month	167 years
$1,000 a month	84 years
$1,500 a month	56 years

*This assumes no investment growth.

If you save $200/mo. at 10% interest	If you save $500/mo. at 10% interest	If you save $700/mo. at 10% interest	If you save $1000/mo. at 10% interest
$15,781	$39,206	$54,822	$78,247
$41,581	$103,547	$144,857	$206,823
$457,849	$1,141,646	$1,597,511	$2,281,309

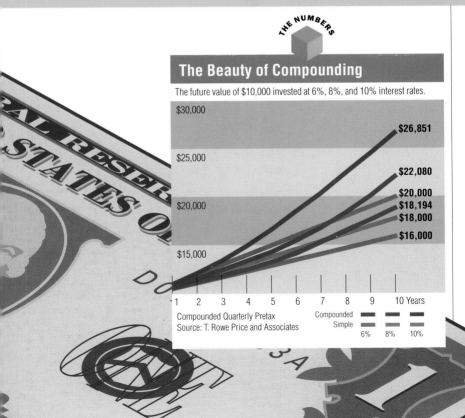

THE NUMBERS

The Beauty of Compounding

The future value of $10,000 invested at 6%, 8%, and 10% interest rates.

$30,000

$26,851

$25,000

$22,080

$20,000
$18,194
$18,000

$20,000

$16,000

$15,000

1 2 3 4 5 6 7 8 9 10 Years

Compounded Quarterly Pretax
Source: T. Rowe Price and Associates

Compounded
Simple

6% 8% 10%

A Guide to the Experts

Appraisers

What They Do
Verify, identify and evaluate property such as art, antiques, real estate

When You Need Them
To certify value of a charitable donation, estate, or property for sale

Credentials
None required

How to Find Them
By recommendation; auction houses often have "appraisal days." Appraisers Association of America 60 E. 42nd St.
New York, NY 10165
212-867-9775
Will give referrals

How They Charge
By hour, day, or job

What to Watch Out For
Unscrupulous appraisers may charge a percentage of the value they assign your goods

Certified Public Accountants

What They Do
File tax returns, represent clients in case of IRS audit, do tax planning; may recommend such investments as limited partnerships, prepare audited financial statements

When You Need Them
To file complicated tax returns and follow up with IRS, if necessary; to structure finances to minimize taxes; to provide audited statements as backup for business loans

Credentials
To use the credential CPA, an accountant must pass an intensive licensing exam

How to Find Them
By recommendation

How They Charge
By the hour. Expect to pay several hundred dollars or more for a tax return

What to Watch Out For
When accountants run afoul of the IRS, all their clients may get audits

Enrolled Agents

What They Do
Prepare tax returns, represent clients in case of IRS audit

When You Need Them
To prepare moderately complex tax returns

Credentials
Enrolled agents must pass a 4-part test to receive their license from the IRS

How to Find Them
By recommendation; many advertise

How They Charge
By the hour

What to Watch Out For
Same as accountants

Estate Attorneys

What They Do
Specialize in preparation and execution of wills and trusts

When You Need Them
To write and/or review a will and to create trusts. Also, to serve as trustees or as executors of complicated estates

Credentials
"General practice" attorneys are perfectly adequate for simple wills, but for trusts, check to see whether the attorney is a member of the American College of Trust and Estate Counsel

How to Find Them
State bar associations list attorneys by specialty. Ask CPAs or lawyers for names

How They Charge
By the hour; top lawyers may charge $400 or more per hour.

What to Watch Out For
With complicated estates, seek out attorneys who actually administer estates, and so know about potential trouble areas

Financial Planners

What They Do
Compile and analyze information about entire financial picture, including investments, insurance, taxes, even budgeting

When You Need Them
For education and retirement planning; to create long-term saving and investment strategies

Credentials
None required. CFP stands for Certified Financial Planner: Planner has passed an advanced course. CLU stands for Chartered Life Underwriter, indicating expertise in life insurance. Planners may also be lawyers, stockbrokers, or accountants

How to Find Them
International Association for Financial Planning (800-945-IAFP) will refer you to 5 local planners, also publishes registry of nation's top planners

How They Charge
Planners may charge by the hour, may charge commissions on investments they purchase for clients, or a combination

What to Watch Out For
Lack of regulation means some planners are underqualified. Commission planners may steer clients to vehicles that pay them best

Insurance Agents

What They Do
Sell insurance policies; aid in processing claims, evaluate insurance needs

When You Need Them
To purchase new insurance or to indicate whether existing coverage is sufficient

Credentials
CLU stands for Chartered Life Underwriter, which indicates expertise in life insurance

How to Find Them
By recommendation

How They Charge
Agent's commission included in insurance premiums

14

What to Watch Out For
Check whether agents are independent or tied to a single company. An agent that represents many insurance companies can offer a wide range of policies

Money Managers

What They Do
Select, purchase, and monitor investments, with or without active participation of client. May also attend to personal bookkeeping, pay clients' bills, and create a budget

When You Need Them
Individuals who travel often, have irregular incomes, or have large sums (typically $1 million plus) to invest may benefit from the close attention paid by a personal manager

Credentials
May have an MBA or CPA, more often not

How to Find Them
By recommendation. A reputable manager will furnish audited performance statistics on request

How They Charge
Generally, 1% to 2% of portfolio's value annually plus trading costs

What to Watch Out For
Dishonest managers have cost clients millions because of incompetence and fraud

Private Bankers

What They Do
Similar to money managers, but do not personally select investments or handle client's affairs; those functions are performed by other departments and coordinated by bankers. Also can extend credit and mortgages

When You Need Them
Individuals with substantial wealth to manage who don't want to do it themselves

Credentials
None required

How to Find Them
Audited performance statistics are available on request

What to Watch Out For
Some banks' investment departments are chronic underachievers

Real Estate Attorneys

What They Do
Review and evaluate contracts for residential or commercial real estate; write leases; advise on zoning, building code regulations

When You Need Them
When buying or selling real estate, renting property, applying for zoning variances

Credentials
Local lawyers are usually qualified—and may be more knowledgeable about the community than a specialist

How to Find Them
By recommendation. State bar associations list members by specialty

How They Charge
By the hour. Top lawyers may charge $450 and up

What to Watch Out For
Landlords and other investors with potential liability should check that lawyer handles litigation as well as contracts

Stockbrokers

What They Do
Buy and sell securities, including stocks, bonds, limited partnerships, options, futures, CDs and more. May also give investment advice

When You Need Them
When purchasing or selling financial instruments; when looking for investment recommendations

Credentials
Brokers must pass exams and register with the Securities and Exchange Commission

How to Find Them
By recommendation

How They Charge
Commissions for every trade; some vehicles have fees built into purchase price

What to Watch Out For
Incompetent or inattentive brokers can help make a small fortune out of a large one, as can "churning": trading stocks just to create revenue for the broker

Tax Attorneys

What They Do
Advise upon and prepare tax returns; represent clients at IRS audits; can appeal audits or represent clients in Tax Court. Also evaluate tax-advantaged investments

When You Need Them
These are taxes' top guns, needed for court cases and big-money deals

Credentials
Although tax law is a very specialized field, there are no specific credentials to signify an expert. A tax attorney should, however, have advanced academic degrees in taxation

How to Find Them
Through state bar or by recommendation. State bar associations list members by specialty

How They Charge
Hourly fees may run to $450 or more

What to Watch Out For
Check that attorney handles IRS hassles, litigation personally

Tax Preparers

What They Do
Complete tax returns

When You Need Them
To do your taxes

Credentials
None required

How to Find Them
By recommendation, advertisements

How They Charge
By the job

What to Watch Out For
Can not represent clients in case of audit

STOCKS

Today, most American adults are stockholders, even if we don't know it. If you own shares in an equity mutual fund, you're a stockholder. If you have a corporate or government pension plan, you may have lots of stock—pension funds have invested over 3 trillion dollars in the stock market, more than any other type of financial institution. So the popular obsession with the stock market, omnipresent in the news we hear and read, and in social conversation, is more than an irritating buzz; it affects almost all of us, albeit indirectly. Stocks represent a big piece of America, and that's why their story makes up the first chapter of this guide.

No matter how bad things look, or how good things look, there is always [a stock] worth buying out there.

Charles Allmon
Money Manager

What is stock, really?

If you think of a corporation as a living being, you can think of stock as its cells—each **share** of stock represents a piece of the whole. When you buy shares, then, you become a part owner of the corporation. And as an owner, you have certain rights: to vote for the company's directors and on issues of importance (such as possible mergers or changes in policy), and to share in that part of the corporation's profits that management decides to distribute (the rest of the profits are yours, too, but will be plowed back into the corporation).

How do people make money with stock?

A stock investor can win 2 ways: when he receives regular, steadily rising **dividends** and when his shares' prices increase. (On the other hand, a stock investor runs the risk that his shares may lose value if the corporation's revenues dive.) Each type of gain is taxed differently. Dividends are taxed as income when you receive them. Shares' price growth, or capital gains, is taxed only when you sell.

Often, investors partake of their gains in the form of dividends, the direct payments corporations send to each **stockholder**. In good years, dividends may rise—and with them, the value of the stock. In bad years, well...the reverse may occur. Many companies, however, reinvest most of their profits to fuel rapid growth. Investors in these firms hope for their shares to gain value in tandem with the growing sales of the firm.

In addition, stock values may be affected by less tangible factors. Share prices are not fixed, but fluctuate according to the **supply** available and **demand**. On the **trading floors** of **stock exchanges** around the world, and over computerized **trading lines**, traders buy and sell at prices that reflect company news, expectations of future performance, rumors both good and bad, economic worries, great press on a new product, even "dumping" by major stockholders who need to raise cash.

World news also moves stock prices. When Iraq invaded Kuwait in 1990, stocks took a dive. But when Operation Desert Storm began in early 1991, sweeping the Iraqis out of Kuwait in a matter of days,

Risk/Reward—Risky in the short term; long term, they tend to beat most other investments.

Liquidity—Most stocks can be sold in a single business day. Even so, plan to stay put for a couple years.

Investment Size—Invest at least $20,000 to get a well-diversified portfolio of stocks.

Attention—Stocks react rapidly to general economic news as well as to specific events.

Goals—Stocks are an all-purpose investment, provided you give them enough time to pan out.

Duration—Experts suggest planning to invest for at least one full market cycle—5 to 10 years.

Tax—As of 1993, both dividends and capital gains are subject to income tax.

52-Week High Low	Stock	Div	Yld %	PE Ratio	Sales 100s	High	Low	Last	Chg.	52-Week High Low
										15 5
										14¼ 12
										12 7
11¾ 9	RJR pfA	.84	8.3	...	2700	10⅛	10	10⅛	− ¼	16¾ 8
23¼ 15½	RLI Cp	.52	2.3	10	42	23¼	23	23	− ⅛	30¾ 2
1⅞ 1⅞	RMI Tl				191	2⅛	2	2⅛	+ ⅛	4⅝
		75e	9.0		81	8⅜	8⅜	8⅜	− ⅛	20¼
		60u	11.4	12	150	5⅜	5¼	5¼	− ⅛	4⅝
						10⅛	10⅛	10⅛	+	4⅝
29¾ 14⅞					83	8		2¼		41⅞
40	ayonr	3.60			8		2			34¾
3⅝	Raytc					2⅛				80¾
29¾ 14⅞	Raythn s	1.30	3.0	9	2104	44⅝	43⅝	43⅞	+	8⅝
47 38½	RdrDg	1.20	2.2	27	706u	55½	54⅞	54	− ⅛	39
55⅜ 40¼	RdrDB n	1.20	2.3	26	72	53¼	53	53	− ¼	76
53½ 42¼	RdeBle s				547	5	d 4¾	4⅞	− ⅜	14¼
9⅝ 5					226	13½	13	13	− ⅛	38¼
17¼ 12¾	REIT	1.28	9.8	10	10	8½	8⅜	8⅜	− ⅛	28¼
19¼ 7⅞	RltRef	1.45e	17.3		378	12⅝	11⅜	12⅝	+	25¾
13¼ 6½	RecnEq				1628	29½	29	29	− ⅛	8
		.30	1.0	1		40		7/32		24⅝

Sym: A stock's symbol is the letters that appear on the ticker (often displayed in brokers' offices and on television news). They may or may not relate directly to the company's name. Anheiser Busch's symbol, for example, is SUDS.

Yld %: Stands for Yield Percentage. Used to compare a stock's yield with that of other stocks and investments.

Vol 100s: Tells you how many shares were traded that day.

Close: Tells you the stock's price at the end of trading that day.

52 -Week Hi/Lo: Tells a stock's highest and lowest prices during the previous 52 weeks. Using this, you can tell whether a stock is near the top or bottom of its trading range.

PE: The price/earnings ratio shows how a stock's share price relates to its earnings. Used to assess the comparative value of stocks.

Net Chg: Gives the change in price between that day's close and the previous day's close.

Hi, Lo: Tells you the stock's highest and lowest prices of the day. Usually, the difference between the two prices is small.

Div: Dividend is shown in dollars and cents, as well as in percentage of share price. (See the yield column.)

30¾ 20⅞	Repsol									39
6¾ 3¾	RepGyp			10	104	45				29
49¼ 38					550	24⅜				26
26 23¾					15	56⅛	56¼	56¾		30
57½ 49½					9 x636	21⅞	21¼	21½	+ ⅛	39
22¾ 9⅜					3739	8¾		8⅞		26
9⅛ 7⅛	Revco n				61	3		2⅞	− ⅛	
3¼ 2½	Rexene n				1025	17⅛	17	17⅛		
18 14⅛	Rexnrd n				441u	47¼	45¾	47¼	+ 1¾	
46¾ 27⅞	RevRev	.96	2.0	16	1225	50⅞	49⅝	49⅝	− 1⅛	
64¾ 46	ReyMtl	1.80	3.6	32	59	23⅛	23⅛	23¼	− ⅛	
28 18⅛	RhP pfA	1.17e	5.1	...	2	23⅝	23⅜	23⅝	+ ⅛	
30 18⅜	RhonPl	1.17e	5.0		767 x	49⅛	48⅞	49	+ ¼	
69⅜ 44⅝	RPR	.72	1.5	18	x767	22½	22½	22½	− 1	
24 17¼	RiteAid	.55	2.4	15	974	23½	14	14	− ¼	
16¼ 12¾	Rivwdl n				36	14¼	13¾	14	+ ⅛	
14⅜ 10¼	RbtHlf			41	159	14	15/16	1	+ 1/16	
4½ ⅞	RbtCec				12	24	23⅝	23¾	− ¼	
24¾ 20¼	RochG	1.68	7.1	16	475	32⅜	31¾	32⅜		
34 29⅞	RochTl	1.54	4.8	16	230	9⅛	8⅞	9	−	
17½ 8½	RckCtr	1.92	21.3	9	522	26½	25¾	26	+ ⅛	
28½ 22¼	Rockwl	.92	3.5	12	2938	57⅝	57	57⅜	+ ⅛	
59⅝ 35	RoHaas	1.32	2.3	18	1167	11½	11¼	11⅜	+ ⅛	
24¼ 9⅜	Rohr				142	331	12¾	12	12⅛	+ ⅛
	RollnE	.10	.8	23	2243	33⅞	33½	33¾	+ ⅛	

stocks began a rally that lasted, with only occasional pauses, all the way to 1992.

The auction-like atmosphere of the stock market can cause both booms and panics, making stock investing seem riskier than it really is. Over time, the peaks and valleys in a stock's price should smooth into a steadily rising curve. An investor who chooses stocks carefully should find that in the long run—that is, 10 years or more—the value of his shares will have grown considerably, outstripping most other investments and keeping pace with inflation.

How do people buy and sell stocks?

Although technically anyone can sell his shares to any buyer, efficiency dictates that investors employ **stockbrokers**, who are licensed to carry out trades on one or more stock exchanges. Two basic types of brokers, full-service and discount, can both sell and buy stocks, as well as bonds, mutual funds, and other financial instruments, but in addition, full-service brokers offer a wide range of investment advice, hand-holding, and, at times, speedier service. For a price. Going the full-service route can cost more than twice as much as employing a discount broker, depending on the size of the trade. For example, the commission for buying 1,000 shares of a $10 stock would be about $100 through a discounter, but about $300 through a full-service broker. If you are an active trader, though, you can often negotiate a price break on full-service commissions—and it never hurts to ask. Ideally, those who make use of full-service brokers get valuable investment advice in return for the higher commissions they pay, but that isn't guaranteed. Finding a good broker, whose approach is compatible

WHAT IT SAYS

"Fully Valued" means **Expensive**

WHAT IT MEANS

Almost 30% of 2,000 high school students recently polled expected they'd earn between $30,000 and $40,000 after finishing their intended education.

Source: *USA TODAY. Original source: Who's Who Among American High School Students*

with your own, can be as confusing as selecting stocks to invest in. (See *5 Questions to Ask Your Broker*, below.)

How do I know whether I'm buying a stock at the "right" price?

Like houses, works of art, and vintage Ferraris, stocks have no "correct" price. Yet there are ways to find out whether you're getting a good deal. Analysts use several measurements, combined with more subjective insights, to assign value to a stock.

• **BOOK VALUE PER SHARE** takes the current **net worth** of a company (that is, the value of its **assets** minus its **liabilities**) and divides it by the number of shares on the market. If a stock's price is lower than its book value, and there's no looming business disaster depressing its prices, it's a bargain. Recent research indicates that stocks selling at below-average price-to-book ratios outperform the market over time.

• **PRICE/EARNINGS RATIO (p/e)**, also called a **multiple**, is the price of a stock divided by the amount of money it earns per share (listed in its **annual report**).

5 Questions to Ask Your Broker

1. How long have you been a stockbroker?
Three years is the absolute minimum experience you should require, but your best bet is a broker who has been in the business long enough to have weathered a falling stock market as well as a rising one. Don't bother asking your broker how he did in the crash of 1987, though—if you believe what people say now, nobody lost any money.

2. Where do you get your investing ideas?
The best brokers will keep up with analysts and respected advisers from the competition, as well as use their own company's research. If a broker tells you his company does the best research, that really means he's just touting the flavor of the month and not doing any brain work of his own. In addition, a broker

should be willing to dig up information on ideas or products you're interested in.

3. What is your investment philosophy?
This is a comfort-factor question as well as a practical one. If a broker likes his clients to sit on a nest egg of tax-free municipals, and you want to trade options, you're talking to the wrong person—and don't let him snow you into thinking he can keep up with you. And if you want to accumulate a stash of blue chips, but your broker is trying to sell you commodities, find someone who's going to move at your mph.

If you want to trade stocks actively, make sure your broker is in touch with his company's trading desks at the various stock exchanges on a moment-to-moment basis. If your broker is not aggressive, your trades may not be executed as promptly as you would like.

4. How many clients do you have?
A broker with more than 100 clients may not have time to service your account adequately, especially if you're investing less than $25,000. If your broker regularly plugs mutual funds with high fees or doesn't return your calls promptly, you're better off without him.

5. Can you give me 2 or 3 client references?
Even though you may have found your prospective broker through satisfied friends, it's nevertheless crucial to ask for references. (After all, your friends may be more easily satisfied than you are!) Get references and call them, just as you would before hiring an employee for your firm. And if your broker won't provide references, find another.

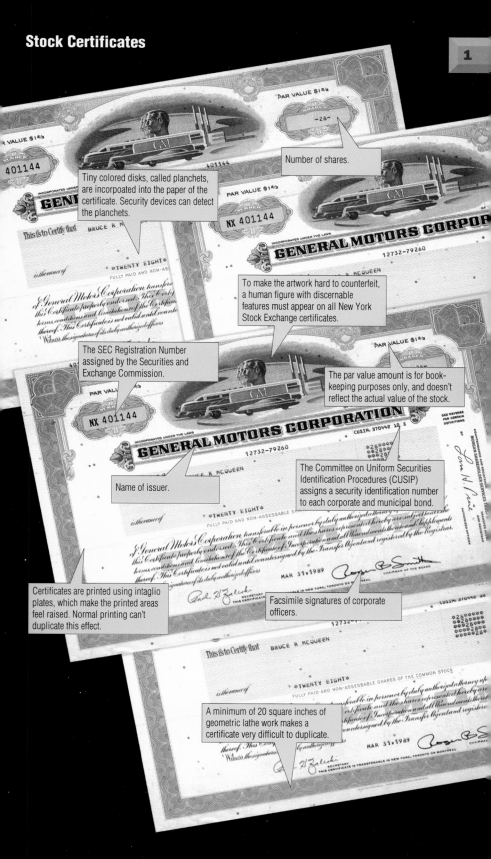

Number of shares.

Tiny colored disks, called planchets, are incopoated into the paper of the certificate. Security devices can detect the planchets.

To make the artwork hard to counterfeit, a human figure with discernable features must appear on all New York Stock Exchange certificates.

The SEC Registration Number assigned by the Securities and Exchange Commission.

The par value amount is for book-keeping purposes only, and doesn't reflect the actual value of the stock.

The Committee on Uniform Securities Identification Procedures (CUSIP) assigns a security identification number to each corporate and municipal bond.

Name of issuer.

Certificates are printed using intaglio plates, which make the printed areas feel raised. Normal printing can't duplicate this effect.

Facsimile signatures of corporate officers.

A minimum of 20 square inches of geometric lathe work makes a certificate very difficult to duplicate.

When a company **goes public**, selling shares to the general public for the first time, its owners have decided that the benefits of sharing their **equity** are worth the pain of parting with some of their future profits. What they get: **capital**, in the form of hard cash, which they can put in their pockets or use to expand.

To issue stock, a corporation must present a **prospectus** revealing the company's history and financial performance, its plans for using the capital it raises, the risks it faces, and the corporate officers in charge. Then investment firms that choose to **underwrite** the stock will assign a dollar value to each share and market the stock to the public. This first sale is called an **initial public offering (IPO)**. In fact, a rash of IPOs is often a signal that the stock market is nearing a peak, and that young corporations are rushing to cash in on the bonanza before it's too late.

For instance, if a stock's price is $25, and it earned $2.50 last year, its p/e would be 10.

Stocks' p/e's are listed in the newspaper along with their price quotes. Conservative investors prefer stocks whose p/e's are less than that of the market as a whole (as of 10/7/92 the p/e for the S&P 500 was 23.71). Exceptions: Issues with very high growth potential, such as high-tech stocks and those in emerging or turnaround industries, often sell at very high p/e's.

• **DEBT/EQUITY RATIO** compares what a company owes to what it owns, by dividing its debt by its net worth. Obviously, a company burdened with monster debts—and monstrous interest payments—is a riskier deal than one that owes little. However, a company that doesn't borrow enough may not have sufficient resources to expand. Usually analysts compare a company's debt/equity ratio with that of others in its industry to see whether its debt load is appropriate.

• **RETURN ON EQUITY (ROE)** tells shareholders how much a company is earning with their money and is listed in its annual report. The ROE is found by dividing a corporation's net income by its capital (the value of money raised through sales of stock plus earnings not distributed to shareholders, or **retained earnings**). A stock should give a better return on equity than alternative investments. In other words, your money should grow faster with a stock than it would with a Treasury bill.

In addition to these numerical guides to a corporation's performance, analysts look for certain fundamental factors, such as strong management, steady sales growth, innovative products, and a profitable, not declining, industry (why invest in a record-manufacturing company, for instance, when everybody is buying compact discs?). Also, many prefer stocks that are priced near the bottom of their typical **annual range** (listed in the newspaper) so there's plenty of room for the shares' prices to grow—a buying style known as **bottom-fishing**.

> *I do not think it is the business, far less the duty, of an institutional or any other serious investor to be constantly considering whether he should cut and run on a falling market, or to feel himself open to blame if shares depreciate on his hands.*
>
> **John Maynard Keynes**

FURTHERMORE

The Dow Jones Industrial Average—What It Really Means

Anyone who listens to the news has heard of the Dow Jones Industrial Average—in fact, to many of us it is synonymous with the stock market. But the Dow is hardly that. Begun by Charles Henry Dow in 1884, the Dow is an index averaging prices of stocks chosen to represent the market, and the economy, as a whole. The first average had just 11 stocks, 9 of which were railroads, reflecting the important role trains played in the stock market then. By 1928, the average had expanded to include 30 industrial stocks, as it does today.

But when the Dow reaches new highs, what does it mean? Certainly the average price of the 30 stocks is not 3,200, even when the Dow is. Although the Dow is called an average, it is more truly an index, representing the historical value of the shares within it since 1928. Stock splits and issues of additional shares by member corporations have affected the way the average is calculated. To see a true average of the 30 stocks' price movement each day, check the percentage change in the Dow, rather than its number.

Dow Jones Stocks

The 30 Dow stocks are worth about 1/4 of the value of all stocks listed on the New York Stock Exchange. These stocks, identified by their ticker symbols, are widely held by both individuals and institutions, and are frequently traded. As a result, the Dow, which is updated every 1/2 hour during the trading day, always reflects recent transactions.

- Alcoa **AA**
- Allied Signal **ALD**
- American Express **AXP**
- AT&T **T**
- Bethlehem Steel **BS**
- Boeing **BA**
- Caterpillar **CAT**
- Chevron **CHV**
- Coca-Cola **KO**
- Du Pont **DD**
- Exxon **XON**
- General Electric **GE**
- General Motors **GM**
- Goodyear **GT**
- IBM **IBM**
- International Paper **IP**
- J.P. Morgan **JPM**
- Kodak **EK**
- McDonald's **MCD**
- Merck **MRK**
- Minnesota Mining & Manufacturing (3M) **MMM**
- Philip Morris **MO**
- Procter & Gamble **PG**
- Sears **S**
- Texaco **TX**
- Union Carbide **UK**
- United Technology **UTX**
- Walt Disney **DIS**
- Westinghouse **WX**
- Woolworth **Z**

Where Stocks Change Hands

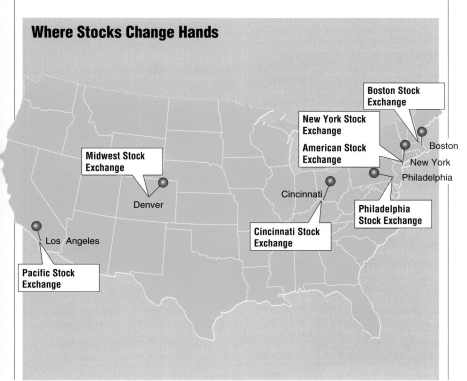

Boston Stock Exchange

New York Stock Exchange

American Stock Exchange

Midwest Stock Exchange

Boston

New York

Philadelphia

Denver

Cincinnati

Philadelphia Stock Exchange

Los Angeles

Cincinnati Stock Exchange

Pacific Stock Exchange

The New York Stock Exchange

When 24 traders gathered to start what is now the New York Stock Exchange on May 17, 1792, they met under a buttonwood tree, where 68 Wall Street stands today. In 1793 they moved to a nearby coffeehouse, and each paid $200 for a "seat"—and they literally meant a reserved chair—as well as the trading privileges that went with it. (In today's dollars, that $200 is worth roughly $1,550.)

By the Jazz Age (1918–1929), seats on the Exchange had become highly prized commodities, selling for close to a half-million dollars ($3,822,265 in today's dollars) each in early 1929. But once the Depression began, their values wilted: in 1935, one could be had for as little as $65,000 ($623,554 today).

During the go-go '80s, prices for the Exchange's 1375 seats once again reached all-time highs, going for as much as $1.15 million before the October 19, 1987 crash. Since then prices have slipped along with investor activity. On July 31, 1991, for example, an NYSE seat sold for $495,000.

DID YOU KNOW?

High Fliers: A Chronology of Speculators' Slang

1800s: Fancy stocks

1920s: High steppers

1950s: Wonder stocks

1960s: Glamour stocks or "Nifty Fifty"

1970s: Story stocks

1980s: Concept stocks

Is all stock-picking so scientific, or does instinct have anything to do with it?

Of course, great investors follow their instincts. But what makes them great is that they follow up their hunches with research, and they know what level of risk they'll take on to go for their projected return. As one highly regarded money manager once said, "I always listen to my instincts. But my instincts are wrong a lot, so I do some investigating before I act."

How do brokers find stocks to recommend?

Full-service brokerage houses have research departments whose job it is to monitor public corporations and make investment recommendations. This is where your broker will get many ideas. The best brokers, however, will look beyond their company's analysts' reports and do additional research on their own before making suggestions. In addition, a good broker will do research on companies or products at your request.

Why do brokers call me out of the blue to pitch stocks?

Brokers' infamous cold calls are somewhere between a public nuisance and a public hazard. Believe me, they aren't calling you with the world's hottest opportunity—if they really had a sizzling property on their hands, they'd offer it to their best clients first, and there would be nothing left for you. Rather, these brokers are usually new to the field, with few or no clients of their own. They sell whatever their company tells them to sell, and they read their spiel from a prepared script. This is hard sell, pure and simple. It has nothing to do with investing, just with pressure to separate you from your money. If a cold caller actually manages to interest you in a stock, ask him to send you written information so you can study it. Don't buy over the phone, unless you know the Force is with you.

THE NUMBERS

What It Costs to Play The Market

Broker	Type of broker	100-share purchase		1000-share purchase	
		@ $10	@ $25	@ $10	@ $25
Merrill Lynch See local listings for phone	Full-service	$50.00	$78.25	$264.60	$428.40
Prudential See local listings	Full-service	$50.00	$79.00	$250.00	$400.00
Charles Schwab 800-435-4000	Discount*	$47.00	$55.00	$110.00	$155.00
Fidelity 800-225-1799	Discount	$46.50	$54.00	$109.50	$154.50
Quick & Reilly 800-926-0600	Discount	$37.50	$49.00	$84.00	$119.50
K. Aufhauser 800-368-3668	Deep discounter*	$24.99	$24.99	$59.00	$70.00
Pacific Brokerage 800-421-8395	Deep discounter	$25.00	$25.00	$70.00	$70.00

* Additional discounts available

FURTHERMORE

Investing Strategies: How the Pros Buy

Stock strategies, like hemlines, go in and out of fashion. Here are some of the classics.

Value investing: First described by the great investor Benjamin Graham (his 1949 book, *The Intelligent Investor*, is still must reading for serious students of the stock market), this is the buying style espoused by such superstars as Warren Buffett and John Templeton. These investors are bargain-hunters at heart. They look for corporations with great products, terrific track records, strong managements, and rosy prospects for the industry. Most important, however, is that a stock sell for far less than it is worth. Value investors assume that the price of the stock will rise once the rest of the world discovers how fabulous the company is.

Growth investing: This style of investing focuses on companies with superior growth rates. The investor is even willing to pay a premium p/e for these stocks because he is convinced that the high growth justifies the price.

Technical investing: Here investors look at the stock's behavior rather than the company's. Technicians often rely on charts that trace the history of a stock price, and are also called chartists. They examine a series of technical indicators, including price patterns, buy vs. sell orders, the amount of cash held by institutional investors, and short interest (the amount of stock held by short-sellers) in an attempt to predict the market's behavior and position themselves to make the most of it.

Asset allocation: Anyone who invests in more than one type of vehicle— such as stocks, bonds, cash, and a house— is an asset allocator, whether he means to be or not. And there's wisdom in this approach: You significantly reduce your long-term investment risks by diversifying your holdings. But strategic asset allocators go one step further, shifting large portions of their portfolios from one family of assets to another to take advantage of market trends. This is a very risky strategy, made more so by its high transaction costs. In the '80s, asset allocators were often called market timers; now, that strategy is somewhat passé.

> *Don't say you love a stock, the stock doesn't know you at all.*
>
> **Edward C. Johnson II**
> Founder, Fidelity Investments

How do you know when it's time to sell a stock?

There are about as many theories about selling stocks as there are investors. Here are a few of the most popular:

- **Sell off your losers.** Rather than let a few lemons drag down your portfolio while you wait to "get even," be disciplined about unloading them. (Of course, some good companies may have temporary downs, which might offer an opportunity to buy more shares.) Pick a level—perhaps a 15% to 20% loss—and let that be your selling cutoff. If you use a discount broker, it won't be too expensive to buy the stock back should its prospects improve.
- **Sell when the reason you bought the stock is no longer true.** If a company didn't introduce the great new product you expected; if it's losing its position as an industry leader; if an anticipated merger doesn't come off—let the shares go.
- **Sell when the stock's price becomes "too high."** If an issue's p/e is significantly higher than that of other companies in its industry, it may be getting overvalued—a good time to take your profits and run.

Stock Performance for the Long Term

As of June 1991:	What a $100 investment is now worth if bought in...		
Stock	1990	1981	1971
Exxon	$123	$735	$2,304
General Motors	$88	$281	$302
IBM	$83	$230	$277
Merck	$189	$1,534	$2,621
Philip Morris	$160	$1,943	$6,768
Consumer Price Index	$103	$147	$333

SOURCES

Here's another way to pick a newsletter—before you invest hundreds on subscriptions, figure out if you can stand reading them.

Select Information Exchange
2095 Broadway
New York, NY 10123
212-874-6408

Selection of 20 financial newsletters (your choice): $11.95

Buying Stock: A Trader's Vocabulary

market order: an order to buy or sell a stock at the going price whenever the transaction is executed. Unless you specify otherwise, this is the way your trade will be completed.

Example: "Buy me 100 shares of IBM At Market."

limit order: an order specifying the highest price you'll pay (if you're buying), or the lowest you'll accept (if you're selling). Limit orders are a good way to trade when prices are moving rapidly, and typically expire at the end of the business day. (You should protect yourself by indicating whether the order is a day order, or whether you want to keep it open longer.) There's one hitch: Set your limit too high or too low, and your trade may not go through.

Examples: "I'll buy 100 shares of Apple today at 50."

"If IBM goes up to 100 this week, sell 200 of my shares."

good-until-canceled order: a limit order that's open indefinitely. This technique is used by investors who want a stock, but only at a certain price. The only problem is, if you forget to cancel the order, you may find yourself the surprised owner of shares you no longer want.

Example: "I want 500 shares of Apple at 40. Make that order good until canceled."

stop-loss order: a form of insurance, these orders instruct your broker to sell shares should they drop to a certain price. Most investors choose a point 10% to 15% below the purchase price, so they're not bouncing out of their stock over a minor fluctuation. Stop-loss orders can do more than minimize a loss; they can lock in a gain, as well. By using a **trailing stop**, investors can arrange for their stop-loss to follow a stock's price skyward.

Example: "Buy me 500 shares of IBM at 95, and enter a stop-loss order at 90. When the stock goes to 100, move the stop-loss to 95."

"Tombstones"

A "tombstone," so named for its funeral type and black border, announces the issue of new stock to the financial community. As well as showing the name of the company, the number of new shares, and their initial price, the tombstone names the companies that underwrite the issue— that is, which buy up the company's shares and resell them to the public.

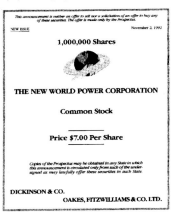

The Investment Explosion: Annual Trading Volume, 1981–90

Along with stock prices, trading volume zoomed in the '80s.

If a newspaper were to list all stocks traded over-the-counter, it would have to use almost all of the pages of a typical issue of the *Wall Street Journal*. Of the 4,206 stocks listed by NASDAQ, only the most active issues are published in the financial pages.

The **NASDAQ Weekly Bid and Asked Quotations** are a weekly summary of other most actively traded OTC stocks. This list, from the *Wall Street Journal*, doesn't go into as much detail as the National Market list, showing only the highest bid and lowest ask of the day.

NASDAQ WEEKLY BID & A...

NASDAQ National Market
"Home of Tomorrow's Market Leaders"

The **NASDAQ National Market** list shows statistics for the most actively traded OTC stocks. Because most OTC stocks are small or start-up companies, few pay dividends. While there is no dividend column, companies that do pay dividends have the amount listed after the ticker symbol.

Other NASDAQ

Other NASDAQ lists a third level of actively traded stocks, (but thousands more don't even get listed). Information here is limited to the highest bid and lowest ask of the day and that day's net change.

Sources: *Investor's Business Daily*, NASDAQ, *Wall Street Journal*

INCOME STOCKS

Although stocks are not primarily an income-oriented investment—you can typically get far better income from bonds—some issues, such as utilities like power and water companies, do throw off substantial dividends. Ideally, these stocks supply a little extra wad for one's wallet while growing steadily in value to keep pace with inflation (something a bond *won't* do).

Are utility stock dividends guaranteed?

No stock dividend is ever guaranteed. Management always has the right to raise dividends, cut dividends, or skip them altogether, depending on the company's profits. Of course, if a company cuts or eliminates its dividend, the value of its shares may dive—especially if it's a high-yielding stock like a utility.

One sort of stock, called **preferred stock**, is less likely to face dividend cuts than the regular variety, also known as **common stock**. Preferred shares often lack voting rights, but do have "first dibs" on a company's profits. Corporate investors, which don't pay taxes on dividends, are the most frequent buyers of preferred stock. Their dividends must be paid before common stockholders see a check. Even preferred stockholders receive dividends *after* bondholders and other creditors are paid, but managers will move mountains to meet the obligation.

DID YOU KNOW?

Bulls vs. Bears

The terms *bull* and *bear* date back to 18th century England. Folk etymology derives *bear* from hunters who collected payment for bearskins before they headed for the woods, then died without delivering the hides. It can be found in print describing investors as early as 1721. *Bull* was probably chosen to oppose *bear* because of the then-popular sport of bull-and-bear baiting, in which bulls and bears fought for bettors' entertainment.

FURTHERMORE

What Is a 'Round Lot'?

When buying stock, investors usually buy in **round lots**— 100 shares or some multiple of 100. Uneven numbers of shares, or **odd lots**, are a lot more expensive to buy and sell: Brokerages charge extra commissions for odd lot trades.

THE NUMBERS

Income From Dividends

Stock	Current yield	Number of consecutive years dividend increased	Dividend growth (10-year average annual rate)
Bristol-Myers Squibb	3.7%	20	18%
John H. Harland	3.7%	39	21%
International Flavors & Fragrances	2.5%	26	10%
Eli Lilly	3.6%	25	13%
Philip Morris	3.4%	24	23%

Pecking Order of Payments

When a company goes bankrupt, creditors get to claim the money owed them in a specific order:

1. Banks and business creditors

2. Bondholders

3. Preferred stockholders (dividends only)

And above all, don't forget the lawyers; they'll make sure they get paid before anyone else sees a cent.

SOURCES

National Association of Investment Clubs
1515 East Eleven Mile Rd.
Royal Oak, MI 48067
313-543-0612

Annual membership/ subscription to *Better Investing*, copy of *Investor's Manual:* $30

A do-it-yourselfers' group, the NAIC has helped hundreds of investment clubs get off the ground. Their publications will not stun you with their wit, but they will give beginning investors a great grounding.

GROWTH STOCKS

A growth stock, as its name implies, is one whose value is expected to grow dramatically over time. The corporation behind it may be large or small, ultra-high tech or decidedly low; what defines this type of stock is that its value comes primarily from its rising earnings and share price and not from dividends. Growth stocks reinvest their profits to speed expansion, rather than handing the cash over to owners. Famous growth stocks have included Polaroid, Xerox, and IBM—companies that pioneered new technology and created entire industries.

To find new growth stocks, advises growth-stock guru Charles Allmon, money manager and editor of the news-letter *Growth Stock Outlook*, seek out firms in expanding industries that have steadily growing earnings (at least 15% a year for at least 4 years), a healthy cash flow, and low or no debt. Then

THE NUMBERS

Growth Stocks—How They Perform

Stock	Average annual return through December 31, 1991		
	1 year	5 years	10 years
Wal-Mart Stores	95.4%	39.0%	46.8%
Coca-Cola	75.3%	37.0%	35.0%
Home Depot	162.2%	80.9%	64.0%

How Growth Stocks Perform Relative to Other Investments
Average annual return through December 31, 1991

Investment	5 years	10 years	25 years
Growth Funds*	13.1%	15.1%	8.5%
Inflation (CPI)**	4.5%	3.9%	5.9%
Long-Term Treasury Bonds**	9.8%	15.6%	7.5%

*Based on an index compiled by CDA/Wiesenberger
**Ibbotson Associates

make sure they're priced right: at close to book value (or less), with a p/e well below that of the market as a whole, and a strong (about 20%) return on equity. Allmon's standards are very high but give the investor an idea of what to aim for.

Are growth stocks riskier than income stocks?

Because growth stocks offer little or no dividend yield, share prices tend to be more volatile than those of income stocks—investors are less likely to hang in there for a dividend check. So these issues may seem riskier, and that's one reason it's important to stack the deck in your favor by buying at the "right" price. Yet over the long term—5 to 10 years or more—a well-chosen portfolio of growth stocks should far outstrip the performance of a more conservatively selected portfolio.

In addition, investing in growth stocks can offset other kinds of risks you take in other parts of your portfolio. For instance, CDs, Treasury bills, and bonds, no matter how safe they may be, have the built-in risk that their **real return**—that is, their gains after inflation has been counted out—may be minuscule. But growth stocks should easily outpace inflation over time, making them an effective counterbalance for even a superconservative portfolio.

What's a blue chip?

A truly stellar stock, with magnificent prospects for long-term growth, a long-standing reputation for paying its dividends, and little chance of loss beyond a transitory blip, is known as a blue chip. Often the company's name is a household word. The term "blue chip" dates from 1904, and refers to the most expensive (blue) poker chips.

The only drawback to investing in blue chips is that some people are lulled into a false sense of security. Blue chips bear watching just like any other stocks.

DID YOU KNOW?

Domestic Purchasing Power

After deduction of taxes and contributions to social security programs, the purchasing power of earnings is highest in Luxembourg, Zurich, and Geneva. Chicago, Toronto, Los Angeles, and Frankfurt are next on the list.

Source: *Prices and Earnings Around the Globe*, 1991 Edition

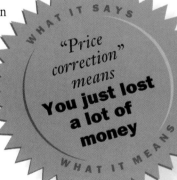

WHAT IT SAYS
"Price correction" means You just lost a lot of money
WHAT IT MEANS

FURTHERMORE

The Recent "Crashes"

The Dow dropped more than 100 points on a Friday 3 times in 5 years: On October 19, 1987, it dropped 508 points; on October 13, 1989, it dropped 190.56 points; and on November 15, 1991, it dropped 120.31 points.

What is an over-the-counter stock?

Many stocks are **listed** on one or more stock exchanges; to be there, they must satisfy minimum capital requirements. (The NYSE's requirement—at least 1.1 million publicly held shares with a minimum value of $9 million to $18 million, depending on market conditions—is the toughest; hence its nickname, "The Big Board.") Many other stocks, though publicly traded, are too small to qualify for an exchange listing. They are sold instead through a computer-linked network of suppliers, called **market makers**, and brokers.

The network's name, **NASDAQ** (pronounced Naz'-dak), stands for National Association of Securities Dealers Automated Quotations. In a sense, it is another stock exchange—the nation's 2nd largest, actually—but one that exists on telephone lines and modems rather than within a building. NASDAQ is so hot lately that some companies that qualify for the Big Board chose to remain on NASDAQ anyway. A few over-the-counter stocks don't even make it into NASDAQ, but are listed by the National Quotation Service, whose daily price lists are known as the **pink sheets**.

They Paid *How Much?*

If you went shopping for a "basket" of 39 food and beverage items in the following cities, this is how much you'd likely pay (in U.S. dollars):

Tokyo	$743
Oslo	$612
Zurich	$517
New York	$476
Paris	$394
Los Angeles	$389
Houston	$386
Toronto	$350
Chicago	$347
London	$301
Hong Kong	$299
Mexico City	$214
Bombay	$116

Note: Based on the average consumer habits of a European family of three. Since items are not specified, this list is of interest as an index reference.

Source: *Prices and Earnings Around the Globe*

THE NUMBERS

Benchmarks for Financial Performance

See how the world can change in a decade.

Dow Jones Industrial Average
- Dec. 31, 1970: 838.92
- Dec. 31, 1980: 963.99
- Dec. 31, 1990: 2633.66

Standard & Poor's 500 Index
- Dec. 31, 1970: 92.15
- Dec. 31, 1980: 135.76
- Dec. 31, 1990: 330.22

In March 1992, a new venue for trading over-the-counter stocks made its debut: **The Emerging Company Marketplace**, a part of the American Stock Exchange. The ECM claims that by placing small company stocks on a physical exchange, they will trade more freely than they do among market makers, leaving them less vulnerable to price manipulation. The ECM opened with 20 stocks (quoted in most major papers at the end of AMEX listings), and hopes to have 50 stocks listed by the end of 1992.

Unlike listed stocks, prices for over-the-counter stocks come in 2 forms: **bid** and **asked**. The bid price is the one a market maker will give you for your stock: in other words, it's the selling price. The asked price is what a market maker wants you to pay for his stock: it's your buying price. The difference between the 2 prices is called the **spread**. When a stock's shares trade very slowly, or **thinly**, the spread will usually be large—a warning signal to potential investors that they may have a hard time unloading a stock at an attractive price.

DID YOU KNOW?

How Much Is a Trillion?

1,000,000,000,000

A pile worth $1 trillion in $1,000 bills would be 63 miles high.

> *Money is always there but the pockets change; it is not in the same pockets after a change, and that is all there is to say about money.*

Gertrude Stein

FURTHERMORE

Who Were Standard and Poor?

Standard & Poor's is the descendant of 2 information-gathering organizations, Poor's Publishing (founded in 1860) and the Standard Statistics Bureau (founded in 1906). Poor's Publishing was the brainchild of Henry Varnum Poor, an expert on the railroads and canals then springing up across the U.S. His investment references were authoritative guides to railroad companies' finances; Poor believed strongly in full disclosure.

In 1906, the Standard Statistics Bureau began publishing financial information on U.S. industrial companies. Like Poor, Standard Statistics' founder, Luther Blake, wanted to improve the quality of information available to investors. In 1923, the Standard Statistics Bureau began rating corporate bonds; it started rating municipal bonds in 1940. In 1941, Standard Statistics merged with Poor's Publishing to form Standard & Poor's Corporation.

THE NUMBERS

Dow Jones? Any Kin to James Earl Jones?

Even though financial scandals and corporate takeovers seem to hit the front page daily, many Americans don't really understand the markets. Oppenheimer Management Corporation surveyed just over 2,000 Americans to find out what they know.

Didn't realize stocks usually do better than popular investments	61%
Didn't have a clue what the Dow Jones Industrial Average was	79%
Didn't comprehend the workings of a mutual fund	56%
Would prefer to discuss family money matters with their spouse than go to the dentist	73%

Source: USA Today

INTERNATIONAL STOCKS

Since "global economy" became an '80s buzz-phrase, investors have begun to buy foreign stocks and other securities at an amazing pace. In 1990, Americans bought over $30 billion worth of foreign stocks and bonds—up from about $5 billion in 1980. Global investing adds an extra dimension to the idea of diversification, the principle of spreading your investments into many areas in order to reduce risk. When you make investments in several countries, you protect yourself against a downturn in any one economy.

What's the difference between investing at home and shipping your money abroad?

Investing internationally can be far more complicated than keeping your money at home. First, stock markets in other countries have significantly different requirements for listed securities, often demanding fewer financial disclosures and maintaining much looser accounting standards. In many countries, for instance, regulations against insider trading and stock manipulation may be as strict as ours on paper, but are not enforced.

Second, an investor in foreign securities is also an investor in foreign currency. Changes in the value of the dollar could wipe out his profits—or, conversely, his losses. For example, if Investor A buys Bonjour Tristesse* stock for 42 French francs, and the dollar is worth 4 francs, he's spending $10.50 a share. Say one year later, the stock is worth 50 francs, and Investor A is eager to sell. The strengthening dollar, however, now worth 5 francs, has not cooperated: if A sells, he will net only $10 a share, a loss of 50 cents.

*The companies named, as well as prices and currency values, are fictitious.

THE NUMBERS

Total Taxes as a Percent of Gross Domestic Product

Sweden	55.3%
Denmark	52.1%
Netherlands	48.2%
France	44.4%
Luxembourg	42.8%
Austria	41.9%
Germany	37.4%
United Kingdom	37.3%
Italy	37.1%
Canada	34.0%
Switzerland	32.5%
Japan	31.3%
Australia	30.8%
United States	29.8%
Turkey	22.9%

Source: *Where We Stand*

DID YOU KNOW?

Although the U.S. continues to outspend other nations on its telecommunications systems, most of its money is spent on maintaining older equipment, while in Europe and Japan, investment is in new technologies.

Now, here's how currency changes can help: Investor B's Satori* stock has plummeted from 14,000 to 7,000 yen. But the dollar has simultaneously sank from 210 yen to 130, cushioning his loss: in dollars, B's buying price was about $67, his selling price, about $54. That's about a 20% loss in dollars, compared with a 50% loss in yen.

Aren't some foreign company stocks sold in America?

Several major international corporations vend securities here, mostly in the form of American Depositary Receipts (ADRs). Most are traded over the counter; the largest are listed on the NYSE or AMEX (see box at right). ADRs are receipts for shares that are held in trust by American banks, which act as administrative go-betweens for you and the firm. They receive dividends and reissue them in dollars, take care of foreign withholding taxes, and do the often substantial paperwork necessary to register ownership of the stock. All in all, ADRs are far more convenient than international stocks for the individual investor.

1

FURTHERMORE

International Investing via ADRs (a small sampling)

Australia
- National Australia Bank Ltd.
- News Corporation Ltd.

Chile
- Compañia de Teléfonos de Chile S.A.

France
- Rhône-Poulenc S.A.

Italy
- Benetton Group S.p.A.
- Fiat S.p.A.

Japan
- Honda
- Matsushita
- Mitsubishi
- Sony
- Toyota

Netherlands
- Philips
- Royal Dutch Petroleum (Shell)

Spain
- Empresa Nacional de Electricidad S.A.

Switzerland
- Nestlé

United Kingdom
- British Airways PLC
- Glaxo Holdings PLC
- National Westminster Bank PLC
- Saatchi & Saatchi PLC

THE NUMBERS

Global Price Comparisons

	Business lunch for 2	Woman's haircut	Alka Seltzer	3-star hotel	Taxi ride 2 km
Atlanta	$15.00	$50.00	$1.43	$139.00	$2.96
Bangkok	$20.58	$12.81	$2.35	$222.45	$1.96
Barcelona	$16.82	$38.31	$2.61	$211.38	$2.47
Houston	$14.00	$29.00	$1.52	$166.00	$3.14
London	$31.30	$45.91	$2.38	$286.96	$4.87
Milan	$42.59	$46.70	$2.79	$222.95	$5.49
New Delhi	$5.46	$4.78	Can't buy 'em	$85.89	$.39
Philadelphia	$30.00	$45.00	$1.70	$180.00	$3.52
Tokyo	$45.00	$65.05	Can't buy 'em	$283.83	$4.04
Vienna	$27.95	$56.30	$2.72	$225.47	$3.74

Source: International Business, December 1991

BONDS

People who are in their 50s and 60s today first learned about bonds when they saved quarters to buy War Bonds (the precursor to today's Savings Bonds) as schoolchildren. Younger people, having learned about bonds from hearing interest rate reports on the evening news, may mirror their parents' inclination toward this simple type of thrift. Even today, when a friend has a new child, or grandchild, the first instinct for many of us is to give a Savings Bond. Lucky baby—she or he, too, owns a small piece of the national debt. ● Bonds of all varieties remain America's preferred investment, perhaps because they seem so predictable. As long as you plan to hold them to maturity, you know how much money you are going to get—typically $1,000—and when you will get it. Bonds seem so stable, so secure.

● And until recently, bonds generally were stable and secure. But the scandalous junk-bond debacle of the '80s, when investors plowed billions into highly speculative issues that were trumpeted as safe (if they were so safe, why were they called junk?), but whose value plummeted as more and more junk-backed firms submerged under their debt; plus the '80s WHPPS disaster (known as "Whoops"), when an AAA-

FURTHERMORE

Bond Prices and Interest Rates

When interest rates rise, bond prices fall.

When interest rates fall, bond prices rise.

rated municipal bond series defaulted because a Washington state nuclear power project went bankrupt, taught us that no investment is perfectly secure. In this debt-overloaded economy, bonds, like stocks, must be examined carefully.

The 1970s underlined another risk: that when interest rates rise, as they did during that decade, the price of bonds falls. Generally, the longer the maturity of the bond, the more its price will fall as interest rates rise.

What is a bond, really?

A bond is simply an IOU—a certificate stating that someone owes you money. When you buy a bond, you buy a debt: you become a lender. All bonds, whether long or short term, corporate, municipal, or federal, work on this principle.

Who issues bonds?

Unlike stocks, which are sold only by public corporations, a great variety of public and private entities can borrow public money and issue bonds. Corporations both public and private can sell bonds; in fact, during the leveraged-buyout (LBO) craze of the '80s, companies "went private"—that is, bought their own stock from the public—by issuing vast quantities of junk bonds.

The U.S. government issues Treasury bills, notes, and bonds to finance the deficit. Interest income from these securities is exempt from state and local income taxes. A few federal agencies—and quasi-federal such as the Government National Mortgage Association (GNMA), the Student Loan Management

> *I personally think the greatest rule in the world is to limit your loss.*
>
> **Alan (Ace) Greenberg**
> Chairman, Bear Stearns

37

Agency (SLMA), and the Federal National Mortgage Association (FNMA), also issue their own bonds.

Because municipal bond interest is tax-exempt, states and cities can pay lower interest rates than corporations do and still offer investors superior after-tax returns. However, unlike federal government bonds, municipal bonds are not necessarily low risk. Enough cities and states are in deep financial trouble for there to be municipal junk, as well as triple-A municipals. Just as lower-rated corporate bonds have to pay extra interest to compete, so do poor-quality municipals.

States, cities, and their agencies sell bonds to raise money for roads and bridges, sewers, industrial development, college dorms, even environmental preservation. They also sell bonds to finance their cash needs between tax collection times. All these bonds are called municipal bonds, even though they don't necessarily have anything to do with cities. Municipal bonds are typically sold in $5,000 or $10,000 bundles and generally are exempt from federal income tax (although certain issues may be subject to a special tax on high earners called the Alternative Minimum Tax, or AMT). Investors who buy bonds from their own state will usually find their interest is also exempt from state and local income taxes—called triple tax-free in investment parlance.

How Corporate Bond Interest Rates Vary by Credit Rating

Based on published yields as of October 1992

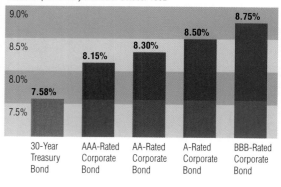

30-Year Treasury Bond	AAA-Rated Corporate Bond	AA-Rated Corporate Bond	A-Rated Corporate Bond	BBB-Rated Corporate Bond
7.58%	8.15%	8.30%	8.50%	8.75%

Source: Salomon Brothers; all corporate yields shown are for industrial companies

U.S. Government Debt

2

Treasury bills: T-bills, as they are better known, have terms ranging from 3 to 12 months. Bills are bought at a discount from their face value of $10,000. The difference between the purchase price and the $10,000 that bill holders receive when the bill matures constitutes the interest.

Treasury notes: Terms run from 2 to 10 years. Notes pay interest every 6 months, just as many traditional bonds do. Notes with terms of less than 5 years have a par value of $5,000; those with terms of 5 years or more have a par value of $1,000.

Treasury bonds: The longest-term debt, bonds can have maturities of as much as 30 years. They pay interest every 6 months and are issued in $1000 denominations.

GNMA bonds: "Ginnie Maes" are issued by a corporation within the federal Department of Housing and Urban Development (HUD), which guarantees pools of home mortgages. Unlike traditional bonds, Ginnie Maes are **self-amortizing**, that is, they gradually pay back principal over the life of the loan (just as the mortgage holders pay both principal and interest). Sold in $25,000 denominations, Ginnie Maes have 25-year terms, but usually last about 12 years. Prepaid, refinanced, and defaulted mortgages in the pool usually cause it to empty out ahead of schedule. Ginnie Maes are not exempt from any form of income tax.

FNMA bonds: "Fannie Maes," issued by the Federal National Mortgage Association, are self-amortizing like Ginnie Maes. Backed by federally sponsored mortgages, they are issued in $10,000 denominations. They are quite safe, but not federally guaranteed like Ginnie and Sallie Maes.

SLMA bonds: "Sallie Maes" work like Ginnie Maes and Fannie Maes, except that they are issued by the federal Student Loan Management Agency and are backed by pools of federally guaranteed student loans.

Bond Certificate

See **Do all bonds have certificates?**, page 40.

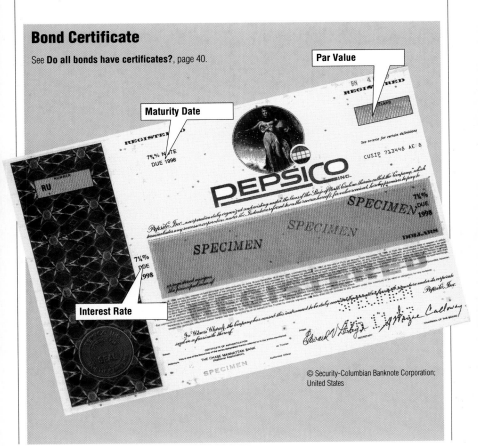

Par Value

Maturity Date

Interest Rate

© Security-Columbian Banknote Corporation; United States

Do all bonds have certificates?

Not anymore. Today, the majority of bonds exist only in electronic form. They are **registered** with the issuer, as well as with your broker. Interest is automatically credited to your brokerage or bank account, instead of being paid in check form upon receipt of your bond coupons.

FURTHERMORE

Bond Quality—A Key to the Ratings

Standard & Poor's	Moody's	Meaning
AAA	Aaa	Best quality, with extremely strong ability to pay interest and repay principal.
AA	Aa	Very strong ability to pay interest and re[ay principal.
A	A	Strong capacity to meet obligations, but somewhat more susceptible to changing economic conditions. An "upper medium" grade.
BBB	Baa	Adequate capacity to pay interest and principal at present, but could be weakened by changes in circumstances. Bonds at this level and above are considered "investment grade."
BB	Ba	Faces ongoing uncertainties or potential adverse conditions that could make it unable to meet its obligations. Bonds at this grade and below are considered "speculative."
B	B	Can pay interest and principal now, but is vulnerable to default in the future.
CCC	Caa	Clear danger of default.
CC	Ca	Highly speculative, may be in default.
C	C	Poor prospects for repayment; bankruptcy may have been filed, but company is still paying interest.
D		In default, or in bankruptcy with debt service in jeopardy.
+, -	1,2,3	Relative ranking within the range of each category. Used on ratings from AA (Aa) on down.

When I bought my bond, I was told that I would receive 10% interest, but on my bond certificate, the interest rate is only 8%. Why is that?

When a bond sells on the open market, its price rises and falls to bring its yield into line with prevailing rates. Rather than selling **at par**—the $1,000 in debt the bond represents—it will sell at a **premium** or a **discount**. Your yield is calculated according to the price you actually paid for the bond: in this case, $800.

Several factors will affect a bond's price. One is the general state of interest rates. Others include the amount of time until the bond matures (the longer the term, the higher the interest), and the economic health of the issuer. The stronger the issuer, of course, the more likely that it will be able to pay both interest and principal on the debt. Weaker issuers, therefore, must pay higher interest rates to win over investors.

An issuer's ability to pay off its bonds is typically judged by at least 2 independent rating services, Moody's Investor Services and Standard & Poor's. Their assessments, from triple A (the best) to D (in default), are the **quality ratings** used to set prices by the bond industry.

What is the difference between current yield and yield to maturity?

Current yield (the type listed in the newspaper) is the rate of interest based on the current price of the bond. You can figure it out yourself by comparing the dollar payment you receive with the bond's purchase price. Yield to maturity, on the other hand, factors in the gain or loss you face when your bond matures and you receive the $1,000 par value, as well as the amount of time until that date. If you bought your bond at a discount, the yield to maturity will include your profit and will be higher than your

SOURCES

Standard & Poor's Bond Guide
Standard & Poor's Corporation
25 Broadway
New York, NY 10004
212-208-8769

Price: $19

Published in January, the annual guide lists quality ratings, rating changes, current yields, and yields to maturity for thousands of corporate and foreign bonds, as well as quality ratings for government and municipal bonds. A monthly guide is also available, for $185/year.

WHAT IT SAYS

"High-yield Bond" means **Junk Bond**

WHAT IT MEANS

THE NUMBERS

How Bond Prices Move With Changes in Interest Rates

Assume you hold a 30-year bond yielding 8%.

If the yield…	Then the price will…
Rises to 9%	Fall 10%
Rises to 10%	Fall 19%
Falls to 7%	Rise 12%
Falls to 6%	Rise 28%

Source: Vanguard Group

current yield. If you bought the fund at a premium, the yield to maturity will include your future loss. Any reputable bond broker can give you an issue's yield to maturity as well as its current yield.

How do I buy a bond? Can I use my regular stockbroker?

Although many bonds are traded on the New York and American Stock Exchanges, in general the system for trading bonds is a great deal more chaotic than that for trading stocks. The majority of bonds are not traded on the exchanges, and their prices are not listed in the paper.

Brokerage houses keep their own inventories of bonds, and sell them to investors at a profit. In addition, they will locate bonds held by other firms for their customers. If you have a good broker, he will use the specialists at his firm to find bonds that suit your needs. If you ask, they will also try to find you the best price among various firms holding similar, or even the

THE NUMBERS

Taxable vs. Tax-Free Yields

It's easy to be tempted by advertised high yields, but this chart shows that it pays to ponder tax implications when shopping for bonds. For example, those in the 28% tax bracket must find a taxable investment yielding 8.33% interest to match the 6% yield of a tax-free municipal bond.

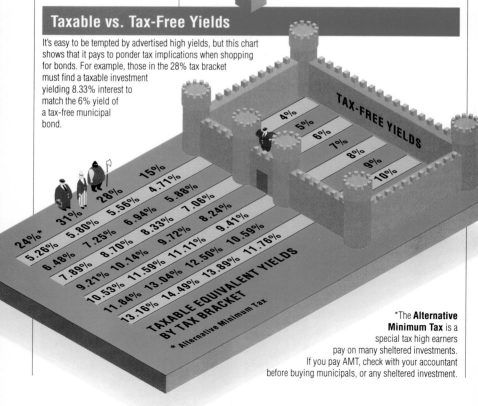

TAX-FREE YIELDS

4%
5%
6%
7%
8%
9%
10%

24%*	31%	28%	15%
5.26%	5.80%	5.56%	4.71%
6.48%	7.25%	6.94%	5.88%
7.89%	8.70%	8.33%	7.06%
9.21%	10.14%	9.72%	8.24%
10.53%	11.59%	11.11%	9.41%
11.84%	13.04%	12.50%	10.59%
13.16%	14.49%	13.89%	11.76%

TAXABLE EQUIVALENT YIELDS BY TAX BRACKET

* Alternative Minimum Tax

*The **Alternative Minimum Tax** is a special tax high earners pay on many sheltered investments. If you pay AMT, check with your accountant before buying municipals, or any sheltered investment.

same, bond issues. You should be specific about the level of safety you desire, and understand that the more highly rated the bond, the less interest it will pay. Also think about the lifespan you're most comfortable with: Long-term bonds may offer higher yields, but come with higher risks of loss due to inflation and to interest rate fluctuations.

Be sure to ask the broker what your bond's **call date** is. Most bond issuers put call provisions in their bonds entitling them to buy out their debt before it matures so they can refinance at a lower interest rate. If a bond is **callable** it has, in effect, 2 maturity dates. Take the early one into consideration, especially when, as now, interest rates are following a general trend downward. In this regard, Treasury bonds are the best bet since they are not callable until the last few years of their life.

How do I buy Treasury bills?

Your broker can sell you **T-bills** for a moderate service charge; so can your bank. Investors can also buy T-bills from the U.S. Treasury at no charge by opening a Treasury Direct Account. T-bills, notes, and bonds bought through a Treasury Direct Account are registered. Interest and maturing principal are electronically deposited in your bank account. Call or write the New York Federal Reserve Bank, 33 Liberty Street, New York NY 10045 (212-720-6619) for instructions on opening an account.

Since 3- and 6-month T-bills are auctioned at the New York Fed every Monday (Tuesday, when Monday is a holiday), you can buy one anytime, either by mail or in person, by submitting a **noncompetitive bid** accompanied by a certified check for the full value of the T-bill (the discount will be refunded to you after the auction). With this type of bid (instructions on submission are available from the New York Fed), investors buy bonds at the average price paid by **competitive bidders**, primarily major financial institutions. Bids that miss one week's auction will be held for the next one.

Twelve-month T-bills, as well as Treasury notes and bonds, are auctioned less frequently. Announcements appear in the financial sections of most major newspapers.

Who Was Moody?

John Moody, a newspaper reporter turned securities analyst, opened his financial publishing firm at the turn of the century. In 1909, **John Moody** developed a system to evaluate and rate corporate debt—from Aaa through C—that is still in use today. He began Moody's Investor Service in 1913.

SOURCES

Federal Reserve Bank of New York
33 Liberty Street
New York, NY 10045
212-720-6310

Publishes a free pamphlet on Treasury Bills.

The Bond Buyer
One State Street Plaza
New York, NY 10004
212-943-8200

Price: $11 per issue;
$1,650 annually

For the serious bond investor, this daily covers the latest bond activity.

Muni Week
1 State Street Plaza
New York, NY 10004
212-943-8200

Price: $14 per issue; $525 annually

Weekly newsletter which covers the municipal bond market.

Department of the Treasury U.S. Savings Bond Division
Washington, D.C. 20226
202-634-5389

The U.S. Treasury publishes several free pamphlets on Savings Bonds including The Savings Bonds Question and Answer Book.

SOURCES

Moody's Annual Bond Record
Moody's Investors Service
99 Church St.
New York, NY 10007
212-553-0500

Price: $48

Published each August, the Bond Record lists new issues, changes in bond ratings, coupons, and call dates for municipal, federal, corporate, and convertible bonds. A monthly bond record is also available. Subscription price: $249/year.

THE NUMBERS

Minutes of Working Time Necessary to Buy...

City	Loaf of bread	Big Mac and large fries
Bogotá	23	98
Chicago	18	18
Hong Kong	14	24
Houston	10	27
Lagos	216	130
London	11	36
Los Angeles	15	20
Mexico City	37	235
New York	22	26
Paris	18	39
Sydney	12	18
Tokyo	14	21
Toronto	10	20
Vienna	12	30
Zurich	9	20

Earnings based on a weighted average for 12 occupations.

Source: *Prices and Earnings Around the Globe*, 1991 Edition

What's the difference between a bond, a bond fund, and a unit trust?

A bond is an individual segment of debt. A bond fund is a mutual fund with a portfolio made up of bonds. Bond funds require less money to start investing, and they can trade their holdings less expensively than an individual can. Funds shield investors from certain risks because of their diversity, made possible by their large size; but some may cut corners on bond quality to keep yields high enough to attract investors, and in the process shoulder more risks than shareholders, as individuals, want to take on. When buying a bond fund, it's important to keep track of the quality of the portfolio, and of the fund's **total return**—a performance report that tracks the fund's yield and gains or losses in its asset value.

Like a bond fund, a unit trust is a pool of money invested in bonds. But unlike a bond fund, a unit trust buys a portfolio and holds it until the trust matures. When the trusts' shares are sold out, it closes to new investors. When interest rates are very high, a trust can lock them in for years. One friend of mine is in a municipal unit trust that pays him 9%, tax-free, until 2003; he bought it in the early '80s when interest rates were sky-high. Now he only wishes he could buy shares for all his children.

When interest rates are climbing, though, trust investors may find themselves trapped in inflexible investments whose returns lag behind those of the market. Although there is a secondary market in unit trusts—and the trust's sponsor will usually buy back shares at the "market price"— the market is limited, so the spread between "bid" and "asked" (selling and buying) prices is wide. This is when the nimbleness of a bond fund is called for—if the fund's managers are lagging behind the market, an investor can bail out with a phone call.

A Bond Owner's Glossary

accrued interest: most people buy bonds partway through an interest period. The interest from the part of the period before they bought the bond—the accrued interest—belongs to the previous owner, and is usually added to the purchase price.

average maturity: the average of the maturities of bonds or other fixed-income instruments in a bond or money-market fund portfolio.

baby bond: a bond with a value less than $1,000, usually $100.

basis point: one-hundredth of 1%. Used in discussing bond yields, as in, "Yields rose 3 basis points today, from 8.25% to 8.28%."

bearer bond: a bond that is held by the "bearer" (that is, owner), who sends in coupons attached to the bond to receive his interest payments. Until 1983, companies kept no records of who owned bearer bonds—unlike registered bonds, whose owners were always logged on computer—making pre-'83 bonds a prized vehicle for laundering cash.

call dates: often companies and municipalities reserve the right to cash in, or "call," their bonds before they mature, so they have the option of refinancing at lower interest rates. The earliest point at which they can pay off the bond is its call date, and appears on the face of the bond.

convertible bond: a bond that can be traded for shares of stock in the company. This conversion feature makes convertibles' prices less interest-sensitive than regular bonds.

coupon: the ticket, attached to the bond certificate, that its owner sends in to receive each interest payment. The coupon rate is the interest rate appearing on the face of the bond.

credit risk: the risk that a bond issuer will not make its interest payments. Assessed by bond-rating agencies Moody's and Standard & Poor's.

current yield: the interest rate a bond yields as a percentage of its current market price—not its face value of $1,000. A bond selling at a discount would have a current yield higher than its yield at issue; a bond selling at a premium would have a current yield lower than its yield at issue.

debentures: bonds that are unsecured—that is, backed by a company's good name but not by specific assets.

default: a bond issuer that doesn't make interest payments, or doesn't pay principal at maturity, is in default.

flat: a bond traded without its accrued interest is flat.

general obligation bond: a municipal bond that's backed by the full faith and credit of its issuer, as opposed to a bond related to a specific project (such as a highway) or agency.

maturity: when a bond's principal is due to be returned.

maturity risk: the risk that a bond with a long maturity will lose market value owing to changes in prevailing interest rates.

par: the face value of a bond, usually $1,000.

pre-refunded bond: a corporate or municipal bond whose issuer has set aside sufficient funds, through a second bond issue, to pay off the first bond at its earliest call date. The second bond issue is normally invested in U.S. Treasury securities. Pre-refunded bonds typically enjoy an AAA rating.

registered bond: a bond whose owner is recorded by the issuer, who pays interest and principal automatically. Often, no actual certificates are ever seen by the bondholder—everything goes on computer. Today, the majority of bonds are registered.

revenue bond: a municipal bond whose interest and principal will be paid with income from a specific project or tax.

sinking fund: money that is set aside for repayment of bond issues and, occasionally, of preferred stock.

spread: when you buy a bond, you don't pay a brokerage commission. Instead, you pay a margin over the broker's own cost. This margin shows up in the spread between the bid (your selling price) and asked (your buying price) prices for a bond.

zero-coupon bond: a bond that does not make interest payments (no coupon, get it?). Instead, it is sold at a deep discount from par and gradually gains value—at its compounded rate of interest—until it matures. If traded before they mature, "zeroes" have more volatile prices than regular bonds.

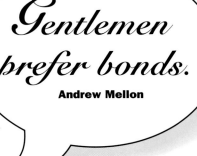

Gentlemen prefer bonds.

Andrew Mellon

MUTUAL FUNDS

Virtually any investment that's legal can be acquired by a mutual fund (provided its rules allow it), which gives investors with small-to medium-sized wallets access to the entire spectrum of investments on the market. The little guy's way into the securities markets, funds pool money from thousands of individuals and invest it all as a gigantic lump sum. ● They may buy vast portfolios of stocks, bonds, gold, foreign currency, options, or several of the latter in combination. They range in philosophy and method from the super-conservative to the ultra-daring. Mutual funds offer individuals (as part of a group) both the diversification and the professional management that they would need hundreds of thousands of dollars to buy on their own. ● Mutual funds are also becoming the friendly neighborhood banks of the '90s. If your fund company is big enough, chances

SOURCES

Investment Company Institute Directory of Mutual Funds

Investment Company Institute
1600 M St. NW, Suite 600
Washington, D.C. 20036

Price: $5

The Yellow Pages of mutual funds, this 207-page book names over 3,000 categorized by type, lists services, charges, and investment minimums, and tells you where to buy shares.

are you can keep most of your savings in a variety of funds there. You can also buy stocks and bonds through its discount brokerage, and the company will issue you a debit card. It may even give you a checking account. Almost all your transactions can be made by phone, often 24 hours a day, and you may be able to invest through your personal computer.

How many shares can a mutual fund sell? Is there a limit?

Mutual funds come in 2 forms: **open-end** (the most common), which issue unlimited numbers of shares that are sold to—or bought from—the public directly; and **closed-end**, which issue limited numbers of shares that are traded on the stock market, as if they were common stocks.

How are mutual funds' share prices determined?

For both forms, price is based on the **net asset value (NAV)** per share, that is, the value of all the investments owned by the fund divided by its number of shares. With an open-end fund, investors pay the NAV for each share, plus commissions if necessary. With a closed-end fund, investors may pay more or less than the NAV (called a **premium** or a **discount**), depending on the popularity of the fund at the moment. NAVs and share prices for most mutual funds are listed in the newspaper.

> *A man is rich in proportion to the things he can let alone.*
>
> **Henry David Thoreau**

Risk/Reward—Funds can be found at all levels of risk and potential reward.

Liquidity—Most mutual funds enable customers to buy and sell shares with a phone call.

Investment Size—Marketed to the small investor, but today many large-scale investors use them as well.

Attention—Stock and Bond mutual funds are a long-haul investment. Money market funds are short term.

Goals—Mutual funds can be found to suit any purpose.

Duration—Mostly for the long term; some can be used to "park" cash for a short time.

Tax—No tax on income from tax-free bond funds. All others taxed.

21 Types of Mutual Funds

The proliferation of mutual funds over the past decade brought with it an ever-increasing variety: Do you want a sector fund, an index fund, a single-state triple tax-free short-term fund? Whatever happened to plain old stock and bond funds?

Aggressive growth

Investments: Stocks, often of companies in emerging or turnaround industries. May use options.

Profit Potential: High. Comes primarily as increased capital gains distributions.

Risk: Very high.

Balanced

Investments: Bonds, preferred stocks, and common stocks. These funds aim to preserve capital, as well as seek both income and growth.

Profit Potential: Medium to high. Interest income (can be reinvested) plus capital gains.

Risk: Medium.

Corporate bond

Investments: Corporate bonds of varying maturities and safety, plus possibly some U.S. government bonds.

Profit Potential: Variable. Income depends on general interest rates and bond quality; share prices rise when interest rates drop.

Risk: Variable.

Flexible portfolio

Investments: Managers can shift from stocks to bonds to money-market instruments, depending on market conditions. Also called asset allocation funds.

Profit Potential: Variable. Depends almost entirely on the fund manager's ability to pick the best markets. Beware of trigger-happy traders. Too much heavy trading can lower returns.

Risk: Variable.

GNMA or Ginnie Mae

Investments: Mortgage securities (pools of mortgages) backed by the Government National Mortgage Association (GNMA). Like bonds, their value can drop if interest rates rise.

Profit Potential: Medium. Share value may rise if interest rates drop. However, you may not enjoy all your potential capital gains because some mortgage holders will pay off their loans early and refinance at low rates.

Risk: Low to medium. GNMA funds are not government guaranteed, although the securities within them are. Also, GNMA prices fall when interest rates rise.

Global bond

Investments: Buy corporate and government bonds from all over the world.

Profit Potential: Medium to high; currency changes, interest changes can raise or lower share values.

Risk: Medium.

Global equity

Investments: Stocks worldwide, including the U.S. Handle paperwork, currency, taxes, and regulatory needs for you.

Profit Potential: High; from stocks, dividends, and currency changes.

Risk: Medium.

Growth

Investments: Common stocks of well-established companies with above-average growth rates. Seek increasing share values rather than dividends.

Profit Potential: High. When the stock market takes off, so do these funds.

Risk: Medium to high.

Growth and income

Investments: A combination of stocks, offering long-term growth with a steady stream of dividend income.

Profit Potential: High.

Risk: Medium to high.

High-yield bond

Investments: At least 2/3 of the portfolio is in low-rated or "junk" bonds.

Profit Potential: Medium to high, primarily in the form of dividend income.

Risk: High.

Income-bond

Investments: A mix of corporate and government debt.

Profit Potential: Medium, in form of dividends.

Risk: Low to medium.

International equity

Investments: At least 2/3 of the portfolio is invested outside the U.S.

Profit Potential: High—managers can go wherever the profits are.

Risk: Very high. Vulnerable to currency swings.

Long-term municipal bond

Investments: Bonds issued by states, cities, and towns. Generally income is exempt from federal tax (unless you have very high income), but may be subject to state tax. Capital gains are taxed at regular rates.

Profit Potential: Low to medium, depending on interest rates, bond quality, and your tax bracket.

Risk: Low to medium.

Money market

Investments: Short-term debt from U.S. government, large banks, and major corporations. The most popular type of fund today.

Profit Potential: Low—interest is slightly higher than a savings account. There are no capital gains.

Risk: Very low.

Option/income

Investments: Buys securities with regular dividends, then augments the income by writing call options on the portfolio.

Profit Potential: Medium, in form of income plus capital gains. But if market shoots up, top gainers may get "called away."

Risk: Medium.

Precious metals/gold

Investments: Typically owns the stocks of companies that mine. Keep 2/3 of portfolio invested in gold, silver, or other precious metals.

Profit Potential: Very low to high, depending on metals prices.

Risk: High.

Sector

Investments: Equities of a specific industry, e.g., utilities, technology, health care. Less diversified than most funds, their share values echo the state of their sector.

Profit Potential: Very high. Because holdings are concentrated in a single area, these funds can really zoom.

Risk: Very high.

Short-term municipal bond

Investments: Short term securities issued by cities and states. Also known as tax-free money-market funds, their interest payments are usually exempt from federal income tax.

Profit Potential: Low. Income only, no capital gains.

Risk: Very low.

State municipal bond

Investments: Portfolios stick to one state, so residents can earn income exempt from federal, state, and possibly city income tax. Also known as "triple-tax-free" funds.

Profit Potential: Low to medium, depending on term of bonds.

Risk: Very low to high, depending on the state's economy.

Stock index

Investments: A portfolio of stocks that mimic the performance of a well-known index, such as the Standard & Poor's 500. Because of passive management, these funds tend to have very low expenses compared with other funds.

Profit Potential: High—mirror the market as a whole.

Risk: Medium to high.

U.S. government income

Investments: Invest in debt instruments backed by feds, including Treasury debt and agency securities like Ginnie Maes.

Profit Potential: Low to medium. Share prices rise when interest rates fall.

Risk: Low to medium, depending on the duration of the debt—the longer the term, the greater the risk.

How do you buy a mutual fund? Is it more expensive than buying stock?

Mutual funds can be bought directly from their companies, at banks, and through stockbrokers. Their fees and annual expenses vary widely. Often funds charge a commission, called a **sales load**, each time you buy shares. Loads range from less than 3% to a legal limit of 8.5%; those that charge the highest commissions typically are available only from brokers. Funds that don't charge a commission are called **no-load** funds. They typically sell shares directly to the investor. But even no-load funds may assess certain fees: **redemption fees**, paid when an investor sells his shares; and a marketing charge, called a **12b-1** fee, that investors pay annually to cover the fund's marketing and advertising expenses. You might say that many self-described no-load funds are, in truth, loaded with hidden costs.

In addition, every mutual fund pays a **management fee** to the investment adviser who manages the portfolio. All these costs can cut into an investor's profits, so it's important to know which ones you're paying before you invest.

How do you measure a fund's performance?

There are 3 ways to look at a fund's progress: (1) track its **share price**, or NAV (Net Asset Value); (2) look at its **yield**— the amount of income it provides; and (3) examine its **total return**—income plus any capital gains or losses after expenses have been accounted for. Each way is important, but the only all-around indicator of a fund's performance is **total return** because it combines the profits from dividends with the profits from portfolio gains, and factors in the fund's costs. This is the number that tells

> *A man is rich in proportion to the things he can let alone.*
>
> **Henry David Thoreau**

you how much your investment dollars are actually growing. When you're comparing one fund with another, especially one kind of fund with another, using total return keeps you from setting apples against oranges.

If you're investing in a **growth fund**, dividends are not important because stocks in the fund will pay little to no dividends. What will be important is a share price that has risen considerably in the past 5 to 10 years. If you're investing in a **bond fund**, on the other hand, yield is extremely important—that's where most of your profits are, as well as, perhaps, the income you plan to live on. But you can't ignore share prices, which may drop if the bonds in your fund's portfolio lose value. Also, some bond funds pump up their yields by buying high-risk debt whose worth may fall dramatically, causing share prices to erode over time.

Who selects the stocks or bonds that my mutual fund invests in?

That is the job of the fund's **portfolio manager**, who makes investment decisions in keeping with the fund's stated objectives (such as capital gains, current income, or capital preservation, for example). Often portfolio managers become stars, as good results garner them a high profile in the media. For example, Peter Lynch, the former manager of Fidelity's Magellan Fund, was worshipped by the press for his spectacular management of the largest equity fund in the country. During his 13-year stint, Magellan Fund investors saw their shares return 2,703.12% (in share value and distributions), while the S&P 500 returned 567.7%. When Lynch retired in 1990, the Magellan Fund had an awe-inspiring $13 billion in assets invested all over the world.

How much money do you need to invest?

Surprisingly, you may need only $500 to invest in some mutual funds, and a couple of fund companies have no minimum investment at all. You can buy shares in virtually any fund with an initial stake of $2,000, and usually can add to your account with as little as $100 at a time.

THE NUMBERS

Mutual Funds' Growing Popularity

Like every other type of investment, mutual funds took off during the '80s, when their numbers grew from 564 at the start of the decade to close to 3,300 today. In 1980 mutual funds had a total of 7.3 billion shareholder accounts (of course, many individuals maintain more than one account), and as of December 1990, there were 39.6 billion shareholder accounts.

FURTHERMORE

Mutual Funds With No Investment Minimum

Twentieth Century Investors, Inc.
4500 Main St., P.O. Box 419200
Kansas City, MO 64141-6200
800-345-2021

This fund company will accept any investment from a customer, even if it's only $1, to start investing in its various stock and government bond funds. However, if your total investment is under $1,000, though, Twentieth Century will charge you $10 a year to maintain the account. (With hope, that sub-$1,000 balance will rise rapidly.) Some other companies, who sell only through stockbrokers, will also require no minimum, but, since you pay the broker a commission, you've got to buy a lot to make the investment worthwhile.

SOURCES

The Mutual Fund Encyclopedia, 1991–92 Edition

Dearborn Financial Publishing, Inc.
520 N. Dearborn
Chicago, IL 60610
800-621-9621 ext. 650

Price: $32.95

An in-depth guide to fund investing, this encyclopedia describes 1,300 no-load and load funds, including performance data, expense ratios, and the styles of funds' investment managers. Author Gerald Perritt, Ph.D., is editor and publisher of The Mutual Fund Letter, *a monthly investment adviser.*

The first public mutual fund was established in Boston in 1924. Before that, all mutual funds were private, and often used for stock manipulation.

SOURCES

What is a Mutual Fund?

Publications Division
Investment Company Institute
1600 M. Street, Suite 600
Washington, D.C. 20036
202-293-7700

This free pamphlet is among others that offer an introduction to mutual funds, dollar cost averaging, and closed-end funds. They also publish a Mutual Fund Fact Book.

How risky is my mutual fund?

Every investment involves some risk (just as not investing does), but the concepts of low, medium, and high risk are vague enough to leave many of us more nervous than we should be. There is an objective way investment risk is often gauged, called the **beta coefficient**, or just the **beta**. It's a number that compares the risk of an investment—such as your soon-to-be-favorite mutual fund—with the risk of the overall stock market.

Here's a description—drastically simplified—of how it works. Analysts compare the activity of a mutual fund over the past year with that of the stock market. If the 2 rose and fell in lockstep—one moving 10% when the other did, for instance—the fund has a beta of 1. A beta of 2 would mean that the fund moved twice as far as the market, in both directions, marking a highly aggressive fund. A beta of .5 would make a fund half as volatile as the overall market. Money-market funds, which don't change share value at all (or aren't supposed to, anyway) have a beta of 0.

Of course, if you're not investing in a stock fund, the beta coefficient is a less helpful guide to a fund's risk. Bond fund values respond to interest rates, not the market; gold funds are tied to the value of gold and, often, world events. So if you're buying bond funds, check out the bonds' ratings and the average maturity of the portfolio, or a similar measure called duration; choose a fund with a duration of less than five years if you want low price volatility. If you're buying gold, just get a crystal ball.

What is a "family of funds"?

In an effort to make themselves seem more human, mutual fund companies with a variety of funds under their roofs market themselves as fund "families." Joining a family gives you a tremendous benefit: Your money becomes very mobile. For instance, if you invest in a stock fund, a bond fund, and a money-market fund through the same family, and you suddenly find you need cash, you can switch money from your stock or bond fund to your money-market fund with a telephone call, then

10 Top Mutual Funds

Virtually any mutual fund can find some way in which it's among the top performers; but the most important question is, how much profit finds its way into your pocket? Here are 10 funds with first-rate returns—after subtracting sales loads, fund expenses, and tax liabilities from both capital gains and dividends.

Fund	Net Assets*	Average Annual Return** 3 years	1 year	Annual Expenses	Portfolio Turnover
Stock Funds					
MIM Stock Appreciation 800-233-1240	$25	19.9%	8.8%	2.9%	240%
MFS Lifetime Emerging Growth 800-225-2606	$255	18.2%	9.3%	2.28%	112%
Wasatch Aggressive Equity 800-551-1700	$12	14.8%	−2.4%	1.51%	41%
Berger 101 (no-load) 800-333-1001	$26	13.0%	9.2%	2.66%	143%
Captial Income Builder 800-421-0180	$926	10.2%	9.3%	0.98%	14%
Global Bond Funds					
Scudder International Bond 800-225-2470	$541	15.7%	20.1%	1.25%	104%
Junk Bond Funds					
Merrill Lynch High Income B 800-637-3863	$641	10.0%	16.0%	1.36%	40%
Mortgage-Backed Bond Funds					
Vanguard Fixed Income GNMA 800-662-7447	$6,101	9.7%	10.6%	0.29%	1%
Municipal Bond Funds					
General Municipal Bond (no-load) 800-645-6561	$932	11.1%	13.2%	0.01%	38%
Treasury Bond Funds					
Dreyfus 100% U.S. Treasury L-T 800-782-6620	$226	9.1%	13.1%	0.56%	21%

*In millions as of June 30, 1992
**As of August 1991, after sales charges
(if any), annual expenses, and taxes,
assuming a 28% rate for both capital-gains
and income distributions

3

DID YOU KNOW?

Although the U.S.'s economy is only twice the size of Japan's, it has 9 times as many billionaires.

Source: *Where We Stand*

Dollar-Cost Averaging

One way people profit with mutual funds is by taking advantage of the low minimum investment to use a technique called **dollar-cost averaging**. To use it, you invest a little bit at a time over a long period—but you always invest the same amount, say, $100 a month. As a result, when share prices are high, you'll buy fewer shares. But when share prices are low, your $100 will buy more shares, bringing the average cost of all your shares lower. As a long-term strategy, dollar-cost averaging makes a great no-discipline savings plan, as many funds will wire money out of your account automatically, at no charge. It also can save you a great deal of money compared with buying shares in a single swoop (unless you happen to buy at a historic low in

write a check. Or if you start getting nervous about your bond fund, say, you can call the mutual fund and move money to another type of fund—maybe equity-income. The best part is that by keeping your money in the family, you can usually avoid paying new commissions when you move your cash between funds.

There are 2 drawbacks to keeping your money in a family of funds. Whereas one family might have a great growth fund, for example, the performance of its other funds may not be so hot. By staying in the family, you could be trading convenience for mediocre performance.

Second, if you shift your money around too much you may be denying yourself one of the great advantages of mutual funds: their value as long-term investments. Ideally, mutual funds should be held at least 5 to 10 years. Although your fund may not have the best growth each year, you should look for consistent growth, year after year, so your investment grows steadily year after year. Many of the funds with

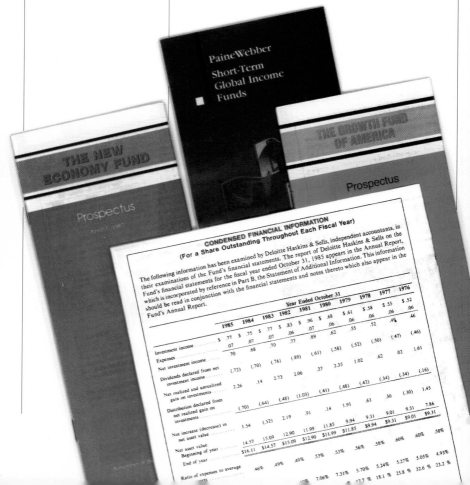

CONDENSED FINANCIAL INFORMATION
(For a Share Outstanding Throughout Each Fiscal Year)

The following information has been examined by Deloitte Haskins & Sells, independent accountants, in their examinations of the Fund's financial statements. The report of Deloitte Haskins & Sells on the Fund's financial year ended October 31, 1985 appears in the Annual Report, which is incorporated by reference in Part B, the Statement of Additional Information. This information should be read in conjunction with the financial statements and notes thereto which also appear in the Fund's Annual Report.

					Year Ended October 31					
---	1985	1984	1983	1982	1981	1980	1979	1978	1977	1976
Investment income	$ .77	$ .75	$ .77	$ .83	$ .96	$ .68	$ .61	$ .58	$ .55	$ .52
Expenses	.07	.07	.07	.06	.07	.06	.06	.06	.06	.06
Net investment income	.70	.68	.70	.77	.89	.62	.55	.52	.49	.46
Dividends declared from net investment income	(.72)	(.70)	(.76)	(.89)	(.61)	(.58)	(.52)	(.50)	(.47)	(.46)
Net realized and unrealized gain on investments	2.26	.14	2.73	2.06	.27	2.35	1.02	.62	.02	1.61
Distribution declared from net realized gain on investments	(.70)	(.64)	(.48)	(1.03)	(.41)	(.48)	(.42)	(.34)	(.34)	(.16)
Net increase (decrease) in net asset value	1.54	(.52)	2.19	.91	.14	1.91	.63	.30	(.30)	1.45
Net asset value Beginning of year	14.57	15.09	12.90	11.99	11.85	9.94	9.31	9.01	9.31	7.86
End of year	$16.11	$14.57	$15.09	$12.90	$11.99	$11.85	$9.94	$9.31	$9.01	$9.31
Ratio of expenses to average assets	46%	49%	49%	53%	.53%	.56%	.58%	.60%	.60%	.58%
				7.06%	7.31%	5.70%	5.24%	5.27%	5.05%	4.93%
				17.7	18.1	25.8	32.6	23.2		

outstanding performance in one year—or even in one quarter—are highly volatile, and may do far less well or even lose money in the year or quarter after their highly publicized gains (ironically, that's when most of us would be buying them).

How do I find out about a fund's policies— its goals, risks, services, and costs?

All these are explained in a fund's **prospectus**, a document that is legally required to describe a fund's activities in detail. The prospectus lists and totals the fund's costs (such as sales charges, redemption fees, and management fees), tells you the fund's objectives and what investments it may buy to achieve them, gives a history of the fund's earnings and expenses, and goes over how one can buy and sell shares. The prospectus may be the most important document you read from a mutual fund—the only competition is the annual report.

Does the prospectus tell me what stocks or bonds my fund owns?

A list of the fund's holdings is in the Statement of Additional Information—part B of the prospectus. You have to ask for it especially, and make sure it has a recent date on it (since funds trade their holdings frequently, you need an up-to-date list). If it's more than a few months old, ask for the fund's latest Quarterly Report.

Most people don't bother finding out what their fund actually owns, but they should. You could discover that a bond fund, for instance, has many high-yielding bonds that are due to mature soon, and will have to be replaced—probably at lower interest rates.

What other services do mutual funds offer?

Even small mutual fund companies now provide an incredible variety of services.

- **Automatic deposits.** If you want to set up a monthly savings plan, many funds will wire money from your bank account, eliminating any need for

SOURCES

100% No-Load Mutual Fund Council Membership Directory

1501 Broadway, Suite 112
New York, NY 10036
212-768-2477

Price: $2

This directory lists only "pure" no-loads—those without sales fees, 12b-1 charges, redemption charges or exit fees, or dividend reinvestment charges. There are just 128 of them out of the more than 3,000 mutual funds sold today. This book lists funds' investment objectives, investment minimums, and shareholder services, as well as the funds' age and size.

3

DID YOU KNOW?

$1,000,000,000,000!

INVESTORS

In January 1990, the total assets invested in American mutual funds passed the trillion-dollar mark.

Average homes in the U.S. cost 3 times more than the average U.S. salary. In Japan, they're 8.62 times more than the average annual salary.

Source: *Where We Stand*

SOURCES

The Individual Investor's Guide to No-Load Mutual Funds

American Association of Individual Investors
625 North Michigan Ave.
Suite 1900
Chicago, IL 60611

Price: members, $19/ nonmembers, $24.95

In addition to information on fund objectives, services, and fees, this guide records funds' past performance and rates how risky they are compared to the market as a whole. Author John Markese, Ph.D., is research director of AAII.

personal discipline. For example, you could have your fund buy $150 worth of shares on the 10th of each month. If $150 a month is too much, some funds will buy you as little as $50 worth of shares every month.

• **Automatic reinvestment.** Your fund can use all your dividends and capital gains distributions to buy more shares, effectively compounding your investment much the way interest compounds in a savings account. Best of all, most dividend reinvestment plans charge no sales commission.

• **Automatic withdrawals.** You can instruct your fund to deposit a certain amount of money in your checking account each month, an option that is most attractive after retirement.

• **Check writing.** Most mutual funds allow you to write checks against your money-market holdings for little or no charge. Unlike bank checks, however, money-market fund checks often have a minimum— $250, for example—and shareholders may be allowed to write only a few checks each month.

• **IRAs.** Most funds allow investors to open IRAs with a considerably smaller investment than they need to open a regular account.

• **Telephone trading.** You can buy, sell, and exchange fund shares over the phone, often 24 hours a day.

• **Wire transfers.** Funds will wire cash into and out of your bank checking account, so you can pay for shares you're buying—or collect for shares you're selling—right away.

How will my mutual funds be taxed?

All mutual fund earnings are taxable as either income or capital gains (unless they have been specified as tax-exempt—and even triple-tax-free funds may earn some taxable capital gains). Any dividends or capital gains distributions you receive should be listed on your return. Profits that remain within the fund—reflected in its higher share price—are not taxed until they are passed on to shareholders. To make your life easier, mutual funds send out tax statements each year.

Taxes get more complicated when you sell mutual fund shares, especially if you've been accumulating them over time. There are 2 simple ways to pay taxes on sold shares, commonly known as FIFO (for "first in, first out") and LIFO (for "last in, first out"). Unless you instruct a mutual fund to do otherwise, it will assume you are selling the first—and usually least expensive—shares you bought (this is FIFO). The IRS will assume this, too, and you will pay taxes on your profits accordingly. Typically, you will endure the maximum tax bite this way. (Keep in mind that you must stick with whichever method you choose.)

To minimize their tax burden for as long as possible, many investors sell shares by the LIFO method. To do so, they must write to their fund and tell it to sell their most-recently-bought shares, listing the dates and amounts of purchase. (It helps to have all your sales confirmations on file.) Then, come April 15, they will only pay taxes on the minimum amount of profit. Of course, they will have to pay taxes on their greatest profits eventually, but the later the better, right?

A third, less often used method of cashing in shares—something of a LIFO subset—is to sell the most expensive ones first, rather than selling chronologically, a good way to go if a fund is very volatile. Of course, this method requires the most thorough filing system.

If you are selling shares within an Individual Retirement Account or other tax-sheltered account (such as a trust), whether you choose LIFO or FIFO does not matter. But in one's taxable affairs, the method of selling you choose can make a considerable difference in the amount you get to keep.

THE NUMBERS

Talking About My Generation

Along with their investment habits, American households have changed dramatically.

Percent of total households	1950	1970	1990
All families	89%	81%	71%
Married, no kids under 18	N.A.	30%	30%
Married, kids under 18	N.A.	40%	26%
Single parents, kids under 18	N.A.	5%	8%
Nonfamily households	11%	19%	29%

Source: Census Bureau

BANKS

In the late '70s, certificates of deposit were earning about 19%. The high returns made everyone look like an investing genius. How could you help but make money when all you had to do was put it in the bank? People's greatest concern was that they not tie up all their cash, because interest rates could go even higher and they wouldn't be able to catch the wave. ● When interest rates finally came down, people became nervous and tried to lock in the best rates they could, for as long as 10 to 20 years. That means some people are just starting to reinvest their high-interest-era profits today. ● With certificates of deposit (CDs) currently yielding as little as 3%—sometimes even less—the main event is not necessarily going to the bank, but, more often, getting out. Fewer and fewer people, it seems, see banks as a primary financial resource. Even robbers "withdrew" 10% less in 1990 than they stole in 1989. ● And yet we still need banks. Where else can you find a checking account and a mortgage and a safe-deposit box? Where else can you salt away cash and know that it's federally insured? ● Although many of the functions banks

> *I don't like money actually, but it quiets my nerves.*
>
> **Joe Louis**

perform are available elsewhere, there is no other institution that performs all of them. So for most of us, a good relationship with a banker ranks up there with knowing a competent broker and insurance agent. In fact, a top-notch banker may substitute for both, especially if you've got a good pile of cash to work with. For "high-net-worth individuals," bankerese for rich people, there's virtually no limit to the tasks a bank will handle. If you're rich enough, bankers may even take care of your pets, *Beverly Hillbillies*-style.

Back on earth with the rest of us, banks are trying desperately to keep customers despite low yields, and they're making a play with convenience. Cash machines, where consumers can get money, make deposits, and transfer funds among accounts anytime, abound. Most banks now house concessions from discount stockbrokers, mutual fund companies, and insurers selling annuities, providing "one-stop" financial shopping and enabling customers to invest in an environment that still, despite the savings & loan debacle, a rash of mergers, and cash-laundering scandals, embodies security and stability.

"Bundled" accounts, which link checking, savings, IRAs, and CDs on a single monthly statement for clients who maintain a minimum balance, are the hot product now. Many banks offer credit cards and premium-rate CDs to these favored customers, whose minimum-balance requirement may be as low as $5,000.

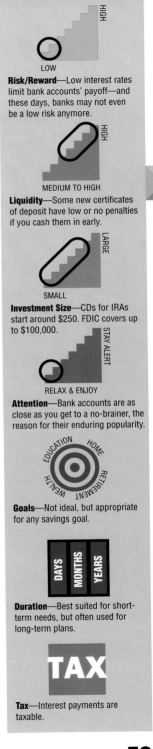

Checkpoints

Risk/Reward—Low interest rates limit bank accounts' payoff—and these days, banks may not even be a low risk anymore.

Liquidity—Some new certificates of deposit have low or no penalties if you cash them in early.

Investment Size—CDs for IRAs start around $250. FDIC covers up to $100,000.

Attention—Bank accounts are as close as you get to a no-brainer, the reason for their enduring popularity.

Goals—Not ideal, but appropriate for any savings goal.

Duration—Best suited for short-term needs, but often used for long-term plans.

Tax—Interest payments are taxable.

4

What's the difference between a bank, a savings & loan, and a credit union?

The term "bank" most accurately refers to **commercial banks**, which originally lent to businesses that wanted to expand, while **savings & loan institutions** lent to individuals who wanted to buy houses and things. Both issued checking accounts, savings accounts, and credit cards to consumers. Commercial bank deposits were insured by the Federal Deposit Insurance Corporation (FDIC); S&L deposits by the Federal Savings and Loan Insurance Corporation (FSLIC) or state agencies for bank insurance.

In the '70s and '80s, though, when banks were deregulated, the distinctions between banks and savings & loans eroded. They both competed for consumers' savings with ever-better deals. They also competed to make loans—to corporations and foreign governments—with over-easy terms. When the businesses didn't pay, hundreds of banks and S&Ls went belly-up and had to be merged or otherwise bailed out by the feds. And there you have it: today's bank and thrift crisis and the enormously expensive rescue.

A **credit union** is not a labor union, although a labor union might sponsor one for its members. It is a consumer-owned cooperative rather than a profit-making corporation like a bank. Most often, credit unions are founded by labor unions or large corporations and are open only to members or employees. They offer competitive interest rates to both savers and borrowers, and most credit unions have federal guarantees backing their deposits.

FURTHERMORE

Federal Reserve Bank Locations

- Boston, MA
- New York, NY
- Philadelphia, PA
- Cleveland, OH
- Richmond, VA
- Atlanta, GA
- Chicago, IL
- St. Louis, MO
- Minneapolis, MN
- Kansas City, MO
- Dallas, TX
- San Francisco, CA

What happens when my bank merges?

As the government has stepped in to combine troubled banks—on top of such major mergers as Chemical Bank with Manufacturers Hanover in NYC, BankAmerica with Security Pacific in California, and NCNB with C&S/Sovran in the South—many consumers are finding that the bank in which they opened their accounts, took their loans, and bought their CDs now has a new name and new policies. Here are some tips to avoid confusion.

- **Chances are, you will get a new checking account and checks.** To simplify your life, the new checks should have numbers starting where your old checks left off. If your bank doesn't notify you when new checks will be printed, ask. Since you'll probably have a new account number (to avoid duplications), double-check your statements even more closely than usual to ensure that deposits are credited to the right account—and that you're not covering someone else's checks.

- **Interest rates on loans and CDs should stay the same.** Other interest rates may change, however, and if a bank is merged because it failed, the acquiring institution does have the right to cancel outstanding CD rates.

SOURCES

Veribanc Instant Rating Reports

Veribanc Inc.
Post Office Box 461
Wakefield, MA 01880
800-442-2657

Price: $10 for first institution; $3 for each additional institution

Veribanc issues safety ratings and in-depth analyses of thousands of banks and S&Ls around the nation. As well as the telephone ratings service, Veribanc issues a newsletter and a variety of reports. For additional information, call 617-245-8370.

4

> *If you would know the value of money, go and try to borrow some.*
>
> **Benjamin Franklin**

THE NUMBERS

Historical Rates on Certificates of Deposit, by Maturity*

Year	3 months	6 months	1 year	1 to 2½ years	Over 2½ years
1984	9.44%	10.07%	10.29%	10.74%	11.06%
1985	7.58%	7.96%	8.28%	8.85%	9.38%
1986	6.28%	6.40%	6.64%	7.00%	7.33%
1987	6.01%	6.23%	6.59%	6.87%	7.27%
1988	6.58%	7.03%	7.40%	7.64%	7.92%
1989	7.96%	8.24%	8.41%	8.41%	8.35%
1990	7.37%	7.65%	7.78%	7.87%	7.87%
1991	5.53%	5.74%	5.96%	6.27%	6.70%
1992**	2.95%	3.16%	3.37%	3.87%	4.62%

*Average effective yield for the year offered by commercial banks on CDs under $100,000.
**Yield at September 30, 1992

Source: Federal Reserve

When Bad Banks Happen to Good People

When the Bank of New England was closed by the feds in 1991, Mary B. (not her real name) bought 100,000 shares of its stock. How could such a gigantic institution not get turned around, she reasoned, figuring that her shares, purchased for 12.5 cents each, had nowhere to go but up. Mary was wrong. The Bank of New England, a bad bank if ever there was one, never got merged. What happened: Its salvageable assets were sold off to a new holding company, leaving a shell corporation with nothing but bad debts. By early 1992, Mary's shares were completely worthless.

Since the savings & loan crisis began in 1978, thousands of banks and S&Ls across the country have been merged, taken over, or liquidated by state and federal authorities. These "bad banks," for one reason or another, could not meet the capitalization requirements the government demands—a set of solvency standards set in response to the last rash of bank failures during the Great Depression. What that means: A bank's capital, or equity, has to equal a certain percentage of its assets (its loans) for it to be legally considered solvent. If a bank's loans went sour, it had to deduct them from its capital reserves, reducing the bank's equity. If enough loans went bad, the bank could go under, and often did.

Although bank stockholders suffer terribly when banks go belly-up, depositors don't, unless they're in a hurry to get their money. If a bank is liquidated by the FDIC, it may take months for a depositor to get his money back. If banks merge, though, things go more smoothly. An account holder may have to acquaint himself with new rules and fees, and send his mortgage and credit card payments to a new address, but for the most part, life will go on as usual.

Before deciding on a new bank, though, a consumer would do well to investigate its financial condition. Any publicly owned bank must provide a copy of its annual report on request. If possible, get a copy of the most recent quarterly report, and take a look at the balance sheet. One key indicator of a bank's health is the number and dollar value of nonperforming loans, which are listed in the annual report. If they're rising rapidly, watch out.

SOURCES

100 Highest Yields

Financial Rates Inc.
Box 088888
North Palm Beach, FL 33408
800-327-7717

One-year subscription, $98;
8-week trial, $34

Although you wouldn't want your checking account to be thousands of miles away from home, there's no reason your CD shouldn't be, if you can earn a better return. This weekly newsletter publishes the highest CD and bank money-market yields among federally insured banks throughout the country. Listings also mention Veribanc safety ratings (see p.61).

Average salary of a bank teller:

New York City	**$28,000**
Paris	**$16,500**
Hong Kong	**$12,200**

Source: *Prices and Earnings Around the Globe*

- **The new bank will issue its own credit cards,** with new interest rates and membership fees.
- **Your bank branch may close.** If both banks have a presence in the same area, they may have branches within blocks of each another. Needless to say, they won't all stay open.
- **Watch your FDIC coverage.** If you had accounts in 2 merging banks and their total, combined, tops $100,000, all the deposits will be insured for just 6 months after the merger is completed. But once the 6 months are up, your coverage will be limited to $100,000 unless you transfer the excess to a joint or trust account.

Why are stockbrokers selling bank CDs now? Can I get a better deal that way?

"Brokered CDs" once had a bad name, because so many of them came from tottering S&Ls. But today, your broker is most likely selling CDs from a major bank or thrift based in an area where competition keeps interest rates higher than the rates available to you locally; 9 of the nation's 10 largest banks sell CDs to consumers through brokerage houses (the sole exception: J.P. Morgan). But some banks are still using brokers to place CDs because they're too weak to attract institutional customers.

If you're thinking about buying bank CDs through your broker, remember that (1) he's charging you a little extra for his trouble, and (2) you may be able to find a higher yield, as well as a more solvent bank, by doing a little research yourself. However, not all brokered CDs are insured by the Federal Government.

FURTHERMORE

The Life of a Check

Every day, millions of checks change hands across the United States. The miracle is that they clear just a few days after deposit, even when they are drawn against banks all the way across the country. (For sums up to $5,000, local checks clear within 3 business days, depending on the amount; out-of-town checks can take up to 6 business days. Any additional money above $5,000 must clear within 9 business days.) The reason money can be transferred so efficiently is that the 12 Federal Reserve Banks act as a clearinghouse, settling accounts between banks more quickly than the banks could do it themselves. In 1986, for example, the Federal Reserve Bank of New York (the Federal Reserve's busiest bank) and its branches cleared 2.2 billion checks with a total worth of $2.7 trillion.

Say you write a check to the Acme Carpet Company of Kalamazoo. When Mr. Acme deposits the check, it joins a bundle of other checks to be deposited at the nearest Fed branch or clearing center, where it is sorted by computer. (The mysterious numbers at the bottom left corner of your check—not your account number—are your routing code.) The Fed that handles Kalamazoo banks then settles your account with the Fed that handles your area—which settles, in turn, with your bank.

Debt is the slavery of the free.

Publilius Syrus
Latin mime writer,
1st century BC

THE NUMBERS

Why People Use Credit Cards

Good for emergencies	75%
Convenient	71%
Safer than cash	47%
Provide extended payments	40%
Can buy things they can't afford now	37%
Good for record keeping	25%

Note: Respondents could choose more than one reason.

Source: *USA Today* 1991. Original source: The Roper Organization poll of 1,223 credit card owners.

SOURCES

Bankcard Holders of America

560 Herndon Parkway
Herndon, VA 22070
703-481-1110

Membership: $18/year

Members can get a plethora of free information, including lists of low-interest and low-fee credit cards, legitimate secured-credit cards for those trying to rebuild credit, a kit for checking up on one's credit record, and booklets on credit and general financial management. Nonmembers can buy this information for a nominal charge.

Although *Chapter 11* is often used as a synonym for bankruptcy, that chapter of the code is for corporations.

PERSONAL BANKRUPTCY

Anyone who's tried to cure insomnia with the television treatment has probably encountered advertisements peopled by men and women with wrinkled brows who are staring at piles of bills. "Maybe we'll have to file for bankruptcy, honey," the man says as the woman rubs his shoulder. Bankruptcy is the last refuge for consumers buried in debt. As painful and embarrassing as bankruptcy can be, it may help individuals hold on to their homes or stay out of jail. But it is truly a last-ditch financial maneuver—it stays in a credit report for 10 years—and shouldn't be undertaken unless you have no other choice.

How does filing for personal bankruptcy work?

Consumers typically file for bankruptcy under Chapter 13 of the bankruptcy code, which covers wage earners with up to $350,000 in **secured** debt (debt backed by property, such as a mortgage or car loan) and $100,000 in unsecured debt. Under Chapter 13, individuals work with the court to create a repayment plan that will erase all their debts in up to 3 years (in some hardship cases, plans may run as long as 5 years). When working out a Chapter 13 payment plan, courts take into account a number of factors, including the debtor's financial situation, length of the plan, employment history and prospects, the amount of debt, any previous bankruptcies, honesty in presenting facts, and any unusual or exceptional problems. Bankrupt individuals will have to write a budget of their income and expenses. Then they must divvy up most or all of the disposable income among the creditors, who may agree to stretch out payments or reduce debts to facilitate the plan.

In Debt Over Your Head? Who Can Help

For those unlucky few who never seem to get ahead of their bills, there is help: The nonprofit National Foundation for Consumer Credit has over 650 credit-counseling services in the 50 states, Canada, and Puerto Rico. Credit counselors help strapped consumers make up budgets, establish bill-repayment schedules, and negotiate with creditors. They may even ask compulsive spenders to destroy their cards. Not to be confused with scammy "credit cleanup" services, Consumer Credit Services usually charge less than $10 a month, and may even be free. All records are confidential. To find the Consumer Credit Service office nearest you, call 800-388-2227.

Worried about your bank? You can get a financial report card from the FDIC's M.I.S.B. Disclosure Group. Information: 800-843-1669 Fee: $2.40

Low-Cost Credit Cards

Low-Interest Cards	Rate	Grace Period	Annual Fee
Arkansas Federal Credit Card Service 800-477-3348	8.00%*	None	$35
Wachovia Bank Card Services (Del.) 800-842-3262	8.90%	25 days	$39
Oak Brook Bank (Ill.) 800-666-1011	10.40%	25 days	$20
People's Bank (Conn.) 800-423-3273	11.50%	25 days	$25
No-Fee Cards			
Oak Brook Bank (Ill.) 800-666-1011	11.90%	25 days	None
AFBA Industrial Bank (Va) 800-776-2322	12.50%	25 days	None
Amalgamated Bank of Chicago (Ill.) 800-365-6464	12.50%	25 days	None
USAA Federal Savings Bank (Texas) 800-922-9092	12.50%	25 days	None

* Variable rate
Source: Bank Rate Monitor; October 1992

What Things Cost in America

	1951	1971	1991
University of North Carolina (tuition, room, board, in-state student)	$3,625	$4,264	$4,948
Harvard (tuition, room, board)	$7,424	$14,170	$22,080
Car (most popular model of that year)	$7,623 Chevrolet Styleline 4-door	$11,741 Chevrolet Impala 4-door	$12,725 Honda Accord DX 4-door
Gallon of gasoline	$1.39 Leaded regular full serve	$1.15 Leaded regular full serve	$1.15 Unleaded regular self-serve
Television	$1,740 Sears 20" B&W Console	$1,436 Sears 21" Color Tabletop	$270 Sears 20" Color Tabletop
Office call with physician (established patient)	$20.48	$28.63	$43.00
Dozen eggs	$3.91	$2.03	$0.94

All figures are in 1991 dollars.
Source: Census Bureau, DYG

RETIREMENT

Now more than ever before, it costs big money to retire. Today, many of us can count on living 20, perhaps 30, years after we pass Go and collect a gold watch. Social Security, the sturdy pillar of our parents' retirement planning, may or may not be available to us—and surely can't be counted on for more than a small share of expenses. Bearing children later in life also means that many of us will be paying college bills during our peak earning and saving years. So our best bet is to take advantage of every opportunity to invest, tax-deferred, through retirement plans. ● Retirement is hardly a financial carbon copy of a person's working life. Some expenses, such as health insurance, may climb dramatically; others, such as commutation tickets and dry-cleaning bills, for soiled ties, may dwindle or disappear. Couples may decide to trade in the family home for a small condo, and use the remaining money to travel. Here is where knowing the realities of a budget can truly make a difference—the better an individual knows where the money goes, the easier it is to plan for a new life after 65. ● Once a person has retired, his need for a personal investing plan hardly diminishes. For once he's made it to 65, he'll most likely live at least another 14 years on average. What that means: Each of us still has to protect our assets against the ravages of inflation, combining conservative, income-generating investments for the here-and-now with such future-oriented investments as equities.

Retirement Options

IRA

Who Can Open: Any employed person or spouse of an employed person can open an IRA.

Tax Deductible? Yes, under limited conditions; in all accounts, gains are not taxed until withdrawal after age 59^1/$_2$.

Maximum Contribution: $2,000 a year per employee; $2,250 a year for employee and spouse.

Keogh

Who Can Open: Self-employed workers, freelancers, and workers for unincorporated companies can open a Keogh.

Tax Deductible? Yes.

Maximum Contribution: 25% of income, up to $30,000.

SEP

Who Can Open: The same workers who can open a Keogh can open a SEP.

Tax Deductible? Yes.

Maximum Contribution: 15% of income, up to $30,000.

401(k)

Who Can Open: Employees whose companies have plans are eligible.

Tax Deductible? Not on your tax return; but deposits in 401(k)s are not counted as taxable wages.

Maximum Contribution: $8,475 a year.

Tax-Deferred Annuities (TDAs)

Who Can Open: Anyone with assets to invest can invest in TDAs.

Tax Deductible? No, but assets' growth is not taxed until withdrawal after age 59^1/$_2$.

Maximum Contribution: None.

Note: TDAs' tax-deferred status is under threat as Congress searches for ways to lower the deficit. Stay in touch with your accountant.

THE NUMBERS

Cashing In Your Nest Egg

After age 70^1/$_2$, the IRS imposes minimum annual withdrawals from your IRA, depending on age and gender. Use this chart to calculate the required *minimum IRA withdrawal.*

If age at withdrawal is:	Divide total IRA account balance by:	
	Male	Female
70	12.1	15.0
75	9.6	12.1
80	7.5	9.6
85	5.7	7.5
90	4.2	5.7

Source: Internal Revenue Service

THE NUMBERS

Vacation Days per Year Around the World

Madrid	32.0
Amsterdam	31.9
Bombay	30.6
Frankfurt	30.1
Panama	28.6
Nairobi	28.5
Stockholm	27.8
Paris	27.0
Vienna	26.8
Rio de Janeiro	26.5
Copenhagen	25.0
Brussels	24.6
London	24.5
Tokyo	24.0
Zurich	24.0
Seoul	23.8
Athens	23.5
Dublin	22.9
Geneva	22.7
Sydney	22.4
Singapore	18.9
Tel Aviv	18.7
Taipei	17.7
Kuala Lumpur	17.6
Bogotá	17.4
Montreal	17.2
Manila	16.9
Buenos Aires	16.2
New York	12.2
Toronto	12.2
Chicago	11.8
Hong Kong	10.9
Mexico City	10.1
Los Angeles	10.0
Houston	9.0

Hours based on a weighted average for 12 occupations.

Source: *Prices and Earnings Around the Globe,* 1991 Edition

INDIVIDUAL RETIREMENT ACCOUNTS (IRAs)

What is an IRA?

An Individual Retirement Account is a special account in which your money can grow, tax-sheltered, until you withdraw it after age 59½. (Before that time, you may take the money, but unless you reinvest it in another qualified pension within 60 days, you will pay hellacious tax penalties that can eat up as much as 40% of your money.) You must start taking money out of your IRA by age 70½. When you withdraw the money, it is taxed at your normal income tax rate. You do not have to pay additional capital gains taxes as you sell off investments in the account.

Even though contributions to IRAs are no longer tax-deductible for many families, growth within the accounts themselves is not taxed until you make a withdrawal—giving you a substantial advantage for long-term growth. So everyone who stopped contributing to his IRA after the tax rules tightened in 1986 should reconsider.

> *Money is something you got to make in case you don't die.*
>
> **Max Asnas**
> Founder, The Stage Deli
> New York City

THE NUMBERS

How Long Will You Be Retired?

The longer you live, the longer you are likely to live, a blessing as long as you have adequate retirement savings. Here's how the clock runs:

Average life expectancy	Men	Women
From birth	71.5 years	78.3 years
At age 30	73.7	79.8
At age 40	74.8	80.2
At age 50	76.0	81.0
At age 65	79.9	83.6
At age 80	86.9	88.7

Source: 1988 life tables, National Center for Health Statistics

I want to move my IRA from a bank CD to a mutual fund. How do I do it?

When your certificate of deposit matures, you will have 2 choices: a transfer or a rollover. With a transfer, you instruct the mutual fund of your choice to collect your money from the bank. The money never touches your hands, so you run no risk of paying tax penalties. However, financial institutions often drag their feet when complying with your request, so if you transfer an IRA, be prepared to follow up.

With a rollover, you withdraw money from your IRA and redeposit it in the account of your choice. The advantage is that you can complete your transaction in a day. The disadvantages are that you can roll over an IRA only once a year (unlike transfers, which are unlimited), and if you don't reinvest the money within 60 days, you must pay income tax on the full amount plus a 10% tax penalty—in total, as much as 40% of the money you withdrew.

I know I have until April 15 to open last year's IRA, but if I postpone filing taxes until August 15, can I postpone contributing to my IRA, too?

No. April 15 is the absolute last day for IRA contributions, no matter when you file.

5

THE NUMBERS

If you have an IRA...

Assume you already have an IRA paying 10% annually, and you are looking to use up your income annually over 5, 10, or 30 years. How much will you get per year?

Amount in IRA	Yearly payout over...		
	5 years	10 years	30 years
$100,000	$ 25,494	$15,858	$10,531
$350,000	$ 89,238	$55,503	$36,858
$500,000	$127,482	$79,290	$52,654

FURTHERMORE

Investments for an IRA

Virtually any investment is eligible for inclusion in an IRA. You can buy certificates of deposit, money-market funds, stocks, bonds, mutual funds, Treasury bills, U.S. gold and silver coins, and publicly held limited partnerships. With a self-directed IRA, you can also trade options and futures. You cannot use IRA money to buy art, antiques, collectibles, real estate (except in partnerships), or precious metals (except for U.S. gold and silver coins).

KEOGH PLANS

What is a Keogh plan?

The self-employed receive many tax advantages in return for their enterprise; one of them is the right to open a tax-deductible, tax-deferred retirement plan called a Keogh. With a Keogh, an investor can set aside 25% of his earned income up to a ceiling of $30,000. And a Keogh contributor can open an IRA as well!

Keoghs have more complicated requirements than IRAs, and may demand a lawyer's help at start-up. Nevertheless, the additional tax shelter can be well worth the trouble. Unlike IRAs, Keogh accounts must be opened in the same calendar year as the deduction you plan to take; however, they don't have to be funded fully until the following April 15.

If I open a freelance business on top of my regular job, which income can I contribute to a Keogh?

You can contribute only income earned as a freelancer. For instance, if you worked at a camera store but also freelanced as a wedding photographer on weekends, you could fund a Keogh plan with up to 30% of the amount you earned snapping happy couples.

If I open a Keogh, do I have to make contributions every year?

Yes, but their size depends on the type of Keogh you have. There are 3 types:

• A **profit-sharing plan** is the most flexible, with an annual contribution that can vary. But its maximum contribution is the lowest—only 15% of earned income up to $30,000.

• A **money-purchase plan** enables you to shelter more funds than other types, but requires that a fixed percentage be contributed every year, even when your business is losing money.

• A **defined-benefit plan** lets you calculate how much income you want at retirement and make annual contributions designed to meet that figure.

Your accountant can help you decide which is the best type for you.

What happens to my Keogh if I close my business?

You no longer have to make contributions, but the Keogh will continue to grow, tax-sheltered, until you begin to make withdrawals after age 59$\frac{1}{2}$. As with an IRA, you must start to withdraw by age 70$\frac{1}{2}$.

FURTHERMORE

Who Can Open a Keogh

- Freelancers
- Employees of unincorporated businesses
- Consultants
- Corporate employees with sideline businesses

5

THE NUMBERS

What Tax Deferral Does to $1,000 Each Year Saved

Source: T. Rowe Price Associates

$270,293

$180,943

$122,346

$99,715

$80,699

$75,585

$63,002

$57,717

$49,423

$38,437

$32,342

$27,299

$19,655

$17,531

$15,645

$11,682

$10,765

$9,924

$7,115

$6,716

$6,336

$4,648

$4,456

$4,272

30 years

20 years

10 years

5 years

8% 10% 12%
Taxable annual return (28%)

8% 10% 12%
Tax-deferred annual return *

* These figures have not been taxed yet, but they will be taxed upon withdrawal.

Working Hours per Year Around the World

Hong Kong	2,375
Manila	2,268
Kuala Lumpur	2,167
Bogotá	2,152
Taipei	2,145
Panama	2,078
Los Angeles	2,068
Bombay	2,052
Singapore	2,042
Tel Aviv	2,015
Houston	1,978
Buenos Aires	1,971
Nairobi	1,958
Mexico City	1,944
New York	1,942
Chicago	1,924
Toronto	1,888
Geneva	1,880
Tokyo	1,880
Zurich	1,868
Seoul	1,842
Montreal	1,827
Stockholm	1,805
Athens	1,792
Vienna	1,780
Dublin	1,759
Rio de Janeiro	1,749
Paris	1,744
London	1,737
Copenhagen	1,717
Amsterdam	1,714
Madrid	1,710
Brussels	1,708
Sydney	1,668
Frankfurt	1,650

Hours based on a weighted average for 12 occupations.

Source: *Prices and Earnings Around the Globe*, 1991 Edition

SIMPLIFIED EMPLOYEE PENSION PLANS (SEPs)

SEPs are a retirement savings option for anyone who's eligible for a Keogh, but SEPs are much easier to maintain. Like IRAs, SEPs can be opened through April 15, they don't demand annual contributions, and they require little paperwork. Like Keogh account holders, SEP depositors can shelter far more than an IRA's $2,000 maximum annual contribution: 15% of income, up to $30,000. And SEP contributions are tax-deductible.

If I open a SEP, can I also contribute to an IRA?

Yes, but a SEP counts as a pension plan, so your IRA contribution won't be tax-deductible unless your adjusted gross income is less than $35,000 if single, or less than $50,000 if married and filing jointly.

FURTHERMORE

SEP Scoreboard

Who can open	Self-employed owners of small businesses and sole proprietors.
Contribution amount	0–15% of earned income; maximum $30,000 (Must be same percentage for all eligible employees)
Minimum annual contribution	None
Deadline for set up	April 15, or same as tax filing deadline
Deadline for contribution	April 15, or same as tax filing deadline
Features	Easy to set up and maintain, inexpensive. Annual amounts may vary. All contributions are tax deductible.

401(k)s

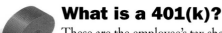

What is a 401(k)?

These are the employee's tax shelter: If your company offers a 401(k), you can save up to $8,475 a year of pretax dollars—often matched by the company with additional funds—which will grow, tax-deferred, until you retire. Its name, hardly melodious, comes from the tax regulation that allows it to exist.

What happens to my 401(k) if I leave my company?

If you change jobs, you can either roll the 401(k) into an IRA, or, in some cases, roll it into your new employer's pension plan.

What kind of investments can I make with my 401(k)?

Unfortunately, your investment options are limited to those that your employer supplies, and you can change investments only during your employer's designated change periods. But that's no reason not to use the plan—the more tax-sheltered savings, the better.

> *I must confess that I am interested in leisure in the same way that a poor man is interested in money.*
>
> **Prince Phillip**

SOURCES

Retirement Planning

American Association of Retired Persons
1909 K St., NW
Washington, D.C. 20049
202-434-2277

Membership: $5/year for anyone over age 55

As well as publishing Modern Maturity *magazine, selling group insurance policies, and offering travel opportunities to members, AARP is a powerful advocate of elderly people's economic rights in Washington. It publishes several free pamphlets, which are available on request. Here is a selection of titles and order numbers.*

A Guide to Understanding Your Pension Plan:
A Pension Handbook
D13533

Look Before You Leap!
A Guide to Early Retirement Incentive Programs
D13390

Planning Your Retirement
D12322

A Single Person's Guide To Retirement Planning
D14185

Are My Social Security Benefits Taxable?
D13539

Mastering Your Money
D14309

Organizing Your Future
D13877

THE NUMBERS

How Americans Feel

Do you think your children will be better off than you are financially when they are your age?

Better off	66%
Not better off	25%
No opinion	9%

TAX-DEFERRED ANNUITIES

Once you've contributed to your 401(k), your IRA, and your Keogh plan, paid your mortgage and your taxes, and set aside cash for emergencies and savings goals, if you have any money left at all (congratulations!!!) you may want to shelter its growth from taxes along with your other retirement funds. The road to this nirvana is usually taken with tax-deferred annuities.

What is a tax-deferred annuity?

Tax-deferred annuities (TDAs) are contracts that allow an investment company (typically, an insurance firm) to invest your money and dole it back to you after you retire. You will need after-tax dollars to buy a TDA (unless you're rolling over another retirement account), but, as with an IRA, the money in the annuity will grow tax-free until it is withdrawn.

The major drawback to TDAs is their expense: Investors may find themselves paying high fees to open the account and high penalties to close it. So be sure that you won't need the money before the TDA matures, and that you've read all the fine print before you write a check.

I'm in the 28% tax bracket and just received a $20,000 inheritance. Should I open a TDA?

That depends on 2 things: whether you have other investment priorities, such as a children's college fund, and whether you need the tax shelter (check with your accountant). As our tax laws become stricter and deductions become more difficult for high earners to claim, TDAs should gain in popularity—that is, as long as their gains remain tax-exempt.

PENSIONS

Those Americans who work for large corporations may find themselves blessed with pension plans, taking some of the retirement savings onus off their shoulders. In most cases a worker must stay in his job a minimum of 5 years to be **vested,** or eligible for benefits even if he leaves the company.

What should I know about my pension?

How soon will I be vested in the plan?
Federal law states that employees must be vested in a company plan once they are employed for 5 years. Some generous firms may vest employees sooner than that, at least partially.

Are Social Security payments deducted from my pension checks? Many plans include Social Security payments in their projections of employees' retirement income. Be sure you aren't overestimating your benefits.

Will my pension checks be indexed for inflation? No. That's one of the many reasons you need other investments. As of this writing, however, Social Security benefits are inflation-adjusted.

What happens to my medical insurance? This varies from plan to plan. You may have to start paying premiums. Be aware, though, that everyone becomes eligible for Medicare insurance at age 65, whether or not he retires.

Our pension is from my spouse's employer. What happens to me if I become widowed or divorced? Unless you have specifically signed away rights to your spouse's pension, you are entitled to it should you become widowed. If you divorce, the pension can be considered a marital asset, and your right to share in it can be negotiated as part of your settlement.

DID YOU KNOW?

$3,000,000,000,000

Value of American pension plans: over $3 trillion

5

SOURCES

Pensions

Pension Rights Center
1346 Connecticut Ave. NW
Washington, D.C. 20036
202-296-3778

A Guide to Understanding Your Pension Plan; $3 plus stamped envelope.

Retirement

Can You Afford to Retire?
Life Insurance Marketing and Research Association
P.O. Box 208
Hartford, CT 06141
800-235-4672

Fee: $1.50

This pamphlet features retirement planning worksheets.

When prosperity comes, do not use all of it.
Confucius

REAL ESTATE

Before stocks, bonds, options, futures, and all that abstract stuff, there was land. Land was the key definition of wealth until the 19th century, when Western civilization became urbanized and industrialized. Even today, owning a piece of earth (or at least a condo) is a more deeply heartfelt goal than virtually any other economic aspiration. ● For most Americans, a home is the most substantial single asset they will ever own. They scheme and save for that first down payment, then lie awake nights wondering whether they chose the right mortgage and what their home will be worth next year. Until recently, they could feel reasonably secure that, over time, their property would rise in value. In a 1960 report by the National

WHAT IT SAYS

"*Speculative*" *means* **You'll probably lose your shirt.**

WHAT IT MEANS

Association of Real Estate Boards, a "luxury home" was defined as one worth $20,000 or more. Reading that now, you might chuckle (if you bought your house in the '60s) or you might weep (if you're trying to buy today).

Whereas in the '80s most of us could count on the value of our homes rising at least as fast as inflation—and in some red-hot areas, a minimum of 15%–20% a year—today homeowners in several parts of the country, especially the Northeast, call themselves smart (or lucky) if their homes' values aren't dropping. Which makes one wonder whether it's time to bargain-hunt and buy or to wait out the storm.

"Prices have dropped dramatically in much of the Northeast during the past few years, but they had zoomed before they started to fall," says Almon R. Smith, executive vice president of the National Association of Realtors. "And in the rest of the country, the market remains firm. In Chicago, Washington, D.C., and most metropolitan areas, for example, median prices continue to rise.

"But don't forget that all real estate is local," Smith says. "A region may be experiencing stagnant prices overall, but some great neighborhoods within it could have healthy growth." The reverse is true too. So it's up to the consumer to get to know the market where he wants to live.

An apartment that costs $5,810 a month in Hong Kong would cost $2,100 in New York City, and $360 in Mexico City.

Source: Prices and Earnings Around the Globe

Checkpoints

Risk/Reward—Low risk, moderate reward provided you're in for the long term. Meanwhile, you get a place to live.

Liquidity—Low. Plan to hold for at least 5 years. Highly sensitive to the economy.

Investment Size—Often the largest investment an individual will ever make.

Attention—Fairly constant need for physical maintenance.

Goals—All 4 goals. Real Estate can be mortgaged for education funds.

Duration—Typically, at least 5 years.

Tax—Capital gains are taxable, but one-time forgiveness available for people over 55 years of age.

6

What are the rules of thumb for choosing residential real estate?

Residential real estate is much more than an investment; it's a home, and will remain so for years to come. So the No. 1 priority is that you have to like it. A lot. In today's housing market, you have to compromise a lot less than you once did.

• **The first rule of real estate is: location, location, location.** This is more true today than ever. Look for an area with good schools, a strong sense of community, manageable property taxes, thoughtful zoning laws. An easy commute to nearby business centers helps housing values, as does access to cultural centers, recreational facilities, and good hospitals. When you find a community you like, go for the best area within it. Owning the smallest, least expensive house on the block is better than owning the priciest.

Median Price of an Existing Single-Family Home in the U.S.

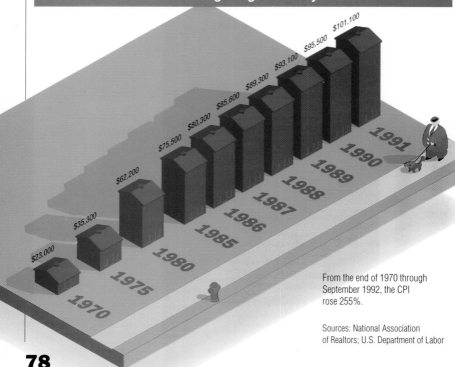

$23,000 — 1970
$35,300 — 1975
$62,200 — 1980
$75,500 — 1985
$80,300 — 1986
$85,600 — 1987
$89,300 — 1988
$93,100 — 1989
$95,500 — 1990
$101,100 — 1991

From the end of 1970 through September 1992, the CPI rose 255%.

Sources: National Association of Realtors; U.S. Department of Labor

78

- **The second rule of real estate is: don't overcommit.** This works on 2 levels. First—don't get in over your head financially. Banks are loaded with foreclosed properties today, seized mostly from dead-in-the-water developers, but also from people who were, shall we say, more optimistic than they should have been. Don't count on a swelling income to cure an overstretched budget in a year or 2. There's no guarantee that your salary will grow fast enough for your needs—especially if you're thinking about going from a 2-career to a 1-career family once you have kids.

How about buying a "handyman's special"?

Don't overcommit yourself to rehabbing a "fixer-upper" unless you're very talented and actually have time to do the work. Gutting and renovating an old building was fine when house prices were on the upswing; today, if you contract out the work you may never make your money back. And for those who can't tell a socket wrench from an alligator clip, "this old house" can be economic suicide.

What types of mortgage financing are available?

When Arthur Miller wrote *Death of a Salesman* in 1949, the mortgage Mrs. Willy Loman set aflame was just about the only type available: of 20 or 30 years' duration, at a fixed rate of interest, usually with a balloon, or large payment of principal, at the end. Mortgage-burning parties were a popular form of celebration in the 19th and early-20th centuries, marking the moment when property truly became one's own.

Today mortgages come in a multitude of varieties. When interest rates are low, consumers often opt for locking in a single, "fixed" interest rate. When mortgage rates are high, "adjustable-rate" mortgages become more popular, partly because banks often offer below-market interest during the first year of the loan.

The key to choosing an adjustable-rate mortgage (ARM) is finding out how, and how often, the rate is adjusted. The majority of ARMs base their rates on

FURTHERMORE

A Mortgage Holder's Glossary

adjustable-rate mortgage (ARM): a mortgage whose interest rate shifts, usually twice a year, to reflect general changes in interest rates.

amortization: paying off the principal (the actual amount lent) of a loan.

balloon payment: a lump sum of principal due at the end of a mortgage term.

cap: a limit on how much adjustable-rate mortgage payments can change. The cap can limit interest charged, or the dollar amount of the mortgage payment.

equity: ownership. When you buy a house, you have the equity represented by the down payment, and the bank, or mortgage owner, has the rest. As you pay off your mortgage, your equity increases.

fixed-rate mortgage: a mortgage with a single rate of interest for its entire term.

point: 1% of the loan. Most banks charge a 2- to 3-point fee to finalize a mortgage.

prepayment penalty: a charge levied when you pay extra on your mortgage before it's due. Today few lenders charge a prepayment penalty.

principal: the actual money lent, as opposed to the interest. Every mortgage payment includes both interest and principal, but the proportion shifts throughout the life of the loan. Your bank can provide a table of payments showing how much of each one is principal and how much is interest.

S O U R C E S

HSH Associates
1200 Route 23
Butler, NJ 07405
800-UPDATES

This organization maintains a list of average mortgage rates for 50 metropolitan areas.

6

When It Pays to Refinance

The '90s have fast become a decade of *rock-bottom interest rates*, and those who bought homes in the '80s are rushing to trade in their mortgages, cutting as much as 6 percentage points off mortgages 8 or more years old. In 1991, for example, approximately 1.5 million households refinanced their mortgages, returning $3 billion to their wallets. In January 1992, according to a survey by the Mortgage Bankers Association of America, more than 70% of the mortgage applications filed nationally were for refinancing, not buying a new house.

If you're considering refinancing, be aware that credit, though cheaper, is tighter than it used to be, and some marginal borrowers no longer qualify for loans they easily could get in the past. Also, your home will be reappraised, and if its value has dropped significantly, you may not be able to refinance the full amount of your mortgage. Most bankers will only write loans to cover 80% of a home's appraised value.

In addition, homeowners who plan to move in less than 5 years may find that refinancing, with its associated costs, is not worthwhile. To calculate whether refinancing is in your best interest, add up all the costs of taking on a new mortgage—reappraisal, points, closing fees, lawyers bills—divide them by the amount of months you plan to stay in your house, and add that number to the new, lower payment. If you *still* end up saving money, sign on the dotted line.

either the interest paid on 1-year Treasury securities or the National Mortgage Contract Rate. Usually ARM interest is adjusted every 3 or 6 months. If interest jumps alarmingly, consumers may be protected by **rate caps**—limits on how much the mortgagor can raise the rate each period, or for the life of the loan. Instead of rate caps, some ARMs may feature **payment caps**, which restrict the dollar amount the loan's monthly payment can rise. The important bit of fine print to watch is that lenders cannot add forgone interest to the principal of the loan.

Most home mortgages today are **self-amortizing**, that is, the loan payments include both interest and principal, so the loan wipes itself out at the end of its term. Owners of cooperative apartments typically find, however, that the mortgage underlying their property (that is, on the entire building) is not self-amortizing. Instead, it has a balloon due at the end of its term that must be paid off or—as is standard—financed again with a new loan.

How do I qualify for a government-guaranteed loan?

Federally guaranteed loans are available to veterans and to first-time homebuyers through both commercial and savings banks. If you qualify, you will probably still have to pay a market rate of interest, but your down payment can be smaller and you'll be eligible for a larger loan than you would otherwise.

What happens if I pay off my loan early?

In most cases, you can save a considerable amount of money by **paying down** your mortgage whenever you have extra money. If you have a **payment schedule** from your bank, listing how much of each installment is principal, you can use it to pay an additional month's worth of principal whenever you have extra money. (In the first few years of most mortgages, most of each month's payment is interest, so a little extra money goes a long way.) Each time you pay an extra month's principal, you lose the need to pay the interest for that month—so a systematic prepayment scheme can save you meaningful money.

By paying one extra month of principal per year, you can pay off a 30-year loan in roughly 22 years. The important detail, of course, is to make sure your loan has no prepayment penalty.

I already own a home but want to make additional investments in real estate. What are my options?

Almost unlimited. You can buy land, a working farm, an apartment house, a share in an office building or hotel—you name it. But before you do, be clear on what kind of time and skill you have to put in and what you expect to get out of the investment. When real-estate values are shaky and the economy uncertain, it's a good idea to research a proposed real-estate investment to death—and do not expect any immediate profits.

SOURCES

The Banker's Secret Bulletin
Good Advice Press
Box 78
Elizaville, NY 12523
800-255-0899

Author Marc Eisenson has turned The Banker's Secret *into a cottage industry for penny-pinchers. The book ($14.95) explains how to prepay your mortgage and save big, as does the software ($39.95); the bulletin ($19.95 for 1 year) ventures into credit cards, taxes, even barter.*

6

THE NUMBERS

Prepaying Your Mortgage—the Eisenson System

Marc Eisenson, author of *The Banker's Secret* (Villard), has devised a system for prepaying mortgages that substantially reduces both the interest you pay and the duration of the loan. To see what his system could save you, see the chart below.

It assumes that you prepay a set amount—$25, $50, $100, or $200—every month for the entire duration of the mortgage. *The amount you save is the total for the entire mortgage.* The months saved is the amount by which the

mortgage term is reduced. So if you have a 30-year, $100,000 mortgage at 9%, and you add $50 to your mortgage check each month, you'll make 78 fewer payments, saving a total of $49,434—that's 6 1/2 *years'* worth of interest.

Prepayment Savings Table for 30-Year Loans

Loan amount	Pre-payment	8% Mortgage Rate		9% Mortgage Rate		10% Mortgage Rate	
		Dollars saved	Months saved	Dollars saved	Months saved	Dollars saved	Months saved
$50,000	$25	$19,951	73	$24,713	78	$30,161	84
	$50	$31,225	118	$37,887	123	$45,248	129
	$100	$44,126	171	$52,548	176	$61,589	181
	$200	$56,415	226	$66,270	229	$76,644	232
$100,000	$25	$23,337	42	$29,441	46	$36,657	50
	$50	$39,906	73	$49,434	78	$60,322	84
	$100	$62,456	118	$75,785	123	$90,496	129
	$200	$88,260	171	$105,108	176	$123,176	181
$150,000	$25	$24,779	30	$31,521	32	$39,633	36
	$50	$44,149	54	$55,304	58	$68,325	63
	$100	$72,952	90	$89,602	96	$108,359	101
	$200	$109,523	139	$131,807	144	$156,091	150

Source: *The Banker's Secret* (Villard Press)

SOURCES

American Bankers Association
1120 Connecticut Ave., NW
Washington, D.C. 20036
800-872-7747

The ABA offers brochures explaining mortgages and worksheets for figuring out how much mortgage you can afford, as well as whether it pays to refinance.

- **You can become a landlord.** Many real estate investors take this route. Some key factors that lead to success: (1) Choosing property carefully, with local rental rates in mind (the rent should exceed the landlord's mortgage plus expenses). (2) Screening tenants carefully. (3) Buying adequate insurance. (4) Being able and willing to do routine repairs oneself, until one owns enough properties to carry the cost of a handyman. (5) Being patient enough to take middle-of-the-night phone calls from tenants with overflowing toilets, blown fuses, etc. Another key: a savvy lawyer, accountant, and insurance agent.

- **You can invest in a real estate partnership.** Partnerships may be private (see Limited Partnerships, page 98) or public, such as master limited partnerships and real estate investment trusts. Public partnership shares are traded like stocks. Private partnerships are much more difficult to sell once you've bought them— the floundering commercial real estate market, plus the loss of most limited-partnership tax deductions since tax reform in 1986, has made them something of a white elephant. The best partnerships today focus on properties with current cash flow, rather than future potential.

> *Private property began the instant somebody had a mind of his own.*
>
> **e.e. cummings**

- **You can buy land.** This is the riskiest way to invest in real estate, unless you have the lowdown on upcoming development. Landowners receive no income from their property but still have to pay taxes, and they may be required to build within a time period stated in the deed. So before they see a penny coming back, land investors lay out a load of cash.

Payments on a $100,000 Mortgage— 30-Year, 15-Year or Biweekly

	30-year	15-year	Biweekly (15-year)*
Interest rate	10%	9.5%	9.5%
Payments per year	12	12	26
Payment size	$877.58	$1,044.22	$522.11
Yearly payment	$10,530.96	$12,530.76	$13,574.86
After 5 years			
Interest paid	$49,228.50	$43,352.53	$41,853.91
Principal reduction	$3,425.61	$19,300.69	$25,499.57
Loan balance	$96,574.39	$80,699.34	$74,500.43
After 10 years			
Interest paid	$96,246.72	$75,027.96	$67,922.47
Principal reduction	$9,061.71	$50,278.43	$67,306.61
Loan balance	$90,938.29	$49,721.57	$32,693.39
After 15 years			
Interest paid	$139,627.74	$87,961.54	$72,266.27
Principal reduction	$18,334.90	$100,000	$100,000
Loan balance	$81,665.10	0	0
Total Mortgage Payments	**$315,928.80**	**$187,959.60**	**$158,721.44**

* Total payoff in 12.69 years
Source: American Banker's Association

6

> *What we call real estate—the solid ground to build a house on—is the broad foundation on which nearly all the guilt of this world rests.*
>
> **Nathaniel Hawthorne**

Owning Their Own

Percent of households owning their own home:

Ireland	82%
Spain	80%
Luxembourg	77%
Norway	73%
Belgium	72%
Japan	60%
United States	59%
Portugal	59%
Finland	58%
Sweden	55%

Source: *Where We Stand*

Average Price of a Home

All figures in U.S. dollars.

Japan	$346,400	United States	$118,100
Canada	$200,000	Australia	$110,000
Italy	$180,000	Netherlands	$99,500
United Kingdom	$135,000	Sweden	$76,000

Source: *Where We Stand*

OPTIONS

The options game—and it is more like a game in its fast pace than are your more standard types of investing— is not for the fainthearted. But for the adept, it is a way to great fortunes. And for the rest of us it can be played in a moderate fashion, either to increase the yield on stocks we own or to reduce the potential for loss in a stormy market. ● Options are the contractual *right* either to buy or sell something, hence, their name. A put is the right to sell something, and a call is the right to buy. The contract includes a strike price—the price per share at which you can exercise the option—as well as an expiration date. If you own an option, you do not have to exercise it. You can merely let it expire—or, if the market goes your way, you can sell the option at a profit instead of exercising it yourself. For

> *Cut your losses, but let your profits run.*
>
> **Bernard Baruch**

SOURCES

American Stock Exchange, Derivative Securities Dept.
86 Trinity Pl.
New York, NY 10006-1881
1-800-THE AMEX

As well as providing general brochures on options investing, the AMEX offers "strategy sheets" explaining various options trading maneuvers in some detail. All are free for the asking.

example, say you bought a 3-month call for XYZ shares at 100 when the stock was trading at 90. The option's **premium**, or selling price, was $300 (or $3 a share) then. After just 1 month, XYZ shares rise to $110. You have 2 choices: You can exercise your option and buy the shares at $100 per share, or you can sell your call, which is now worth $1,300—a quick $1,000 profit.

Although you may have made even more money had you just bought 100 shares of XYZ outright, you would have had to invest $9,000 instead of $300. Which means you could have lost a lot more as well. Options offer the sophisticated and attentive investor the advantages of **leverage**, or making a large transaction with only a small amount of their own money, to maximize profits.

How do you open an option account?

Unlike a standard brokerage account, you need to qualify to trade options. Because certain option strategies entail great financial risks, you will have to show a minimum net worth before your broker can trade options for you. In some cases, you may have to open a **margin account** (an account where you trade with money borrowed from your brokerage) as well. At Merrill Lynch, the trading limit on an options account is pegged to the client's net worth and liquidity.

What's a covered call?

The option strategy used most often by individual investors is writing **covered calls**—that is, selling a call against stock held in the investor's portfolio. The person who buys the call has the right to buy the investor's shares at a predetermined **strike price**; but will not **exercise** the call, taking possession of the shares, unless their value rises to that level or higher.

Checkpoints

LOW — HIGH

Risk/Reward—High, on both counts.

LOW — HIGH

Liquidity—Low to high, depending on the stock.

SMALL — LARGE

Investment Size—From a few hundred dollars to several thousand.

RELAX & ENJOY — STAY ALERT

Attention—Very high. Options prices may change dramatically over a few hours.

WEALTH

Goals—Wealth. Unless you use them to maximize the income from stocks you already own, options are purely for the short term.

DAYS   MONTHS   YEARS

Duration—Contracts go from 3 months to a year, but most are closed out long before that.

TAX

Tax—Profits are fully taxable.

7

Selling covered calls benefits the investor in 2 ways: first, he can make some extra money on the stock. He can also protect himself, to a certain extent, against the stock's possible loss in value. On the other hand, if the stock really takes off, the shares will probably get **called away**, and the investor will have limited the amount of profit he can make.

Say, for example, you own stock in Integrated Potpourri that you bought for $36. (This example does not include transaction costs or taxes.) When IP shares reach 38, you sell a call giving the buyer the right to buy 100 shares (the standard quantity for options) at $40. The option, which sells for $4, lasts 6 months. You've won 2 things: an extra $4 profit on each of your shares, and protection against loss if the stock price falls (since you've already realized $4 per share, you make a profit as long as Integrated Potpourri's price remains above 32). If IP's price shoots up to $42, though, your shares will most likely get called, and you'll miss out on that last $2 per share profit.

Another risk in writing covered calls is that you lose some liquidity. Since you may be obligated to deliver those shares at any point during the option's 6-month duration, you can't sell them off—unless you're willing to **go naked**, a far riskier game, and take the chance that you'll be able to replace the shares, or buy a put to close the transaction, later on.

What Are Your Options?

	Buy	Sell
Puts	You buy the right to sell 100 shares of stock to someone at a specific price and for a set period.	You sell someone the right to sell you 100 shares at a specific price and for a set period.
How you profit	The price of the underlying stock falls. You exercise the option or sell it at a profit.	The price of the stock stays the same or rises. The put expires and you keep the money.
Calls	You buy the option to purchase 100 shares of stock from someone at a specific price and for a set time.	You sell someone the option to buy your 100 shares at a specific price and for a set period.
How you profit	The stock price rises; you take possession of the stock at a discount to market, or sell the put at a profit.	The stock price falls, the call expires, and you keep the premium.

An Option Trader's Glossary

at the money: when a strike price is the same as that of the underlying stock.

call: the right to buy a stock at a specified price.

closing transaction: buying or selling an option to cancel out a previously held position.

covered: an option written against shares you already own.

diagonal spread: simultaneously buying and selling options on the same security, with different expiration dates and different strike prices.

in the money: an option that would make a profit if exercised.

horizontal spread: simultaneously buying and selling options on a security with the same strike price but different expiration dates.

married put: a put on shares you already own.

naked: an option written against shares you do not own.

opening transaction: the sale or purchase of an option.

out of the money: an option that would be unprofitable to exercise.

premium: an option's selling price.

put: the right to sell a stock at a specified price.

spread: buying and selling options on a security at the same time, locking in a closing transaction and limiting your risk.

strike price: the price a stock must reach for the option owner to exercise the option.

vertical spread: simultaneously buying and selling options on the same security with the same expiration dates, but different strike prices.

Gross and Net Hourly Earnings Around the World

City	Level of earnings		
	Gross/hour	Net/hour	% for taxes and Social Security
Zurich	$20.20	$16.00	19.4%
Geneva	$18.80	$14.50	22.5%
Luxembourg	$13.90	$11.40	18.3%
Tokyo	$12.90	$10.90	15.5%
New York City	$13.80	$10.50	22.7%
Los Angeles	$14.30	$10.40	25.4%
Oslo	$16.30	$10.20	37.8%
Frankfurt	$14.60	$9.70	33.6%
Chicago	$14.40	$9.90	31.1%
Toronto	$13.20	$9.30	29.2%
Montreal	$12.90	$9.00	29.8%
London	$9.20	$7.40	18.7%
Paris	$9.70	$7.30	24.3%
Hong Kong	$4.80	$4.50	5.8%
Mexico City	$1.00	$.90	4.7%

Figures based on a weighted average for 12 occupations.
Source: *Prices and Earnings Around the Globe,* 1991 Edition

7

> *The world is full of willing people. Some willing to work, the rest willing to let them.*
>
> **Robert Frost**

PRECIOUS METALS

Yes, Virginia, all that glitters is not gold—it could also be silver, platinum, even titanium, rhodium, or palladium, if you have a taste for the exotic. Precious and strategic metals have long been a part of the sophisticated investor's portfolio, as both a speculative play and, particularly for gold, as a hedge against inflation. ● The general rule of thumb in the case of gold—the favorite precious metal for investing, as it is for jewelry—works like this: When the world goes to pot, gold keeps its value. Hyperinflation, oil shortages, wars—all are occasions in which goldbugs may profit. Here is an investment that is strongly affected by the news, both economic and political. Since

> *The chief value of money lies in the fact that one lives in a world in which it is overestimated.*
>
> **H.L. Mencken**

SOURCES

Coin World
911 Vandemark Rd.
Sidney, OH 45365
513-498-0800

Published weekly, this magazine covers collectible coins from around the world.

the late '80s, however, the calamity scenario has proved less beneficial to metals investors than it did before. The Gulf war, for example, hardly sent gold to the $875/ounce high it reached in January 1980; in fact, the metal didn't even break $400. As the financial futures market gains wider acceptance as a means of hedging—or protecting portfolios of stocks and bonds—gold's value as a haven in troubled times may continue to decline.

Yet other metal investments have had better recent records. Gold-mining stocks, for instance, ran up to record highs in the late '80s. Numismatic gold and silver coins—those coins that have collectible as well as bullion value—have also performed well. For instance, the 1849 Saint-Gaudens $20 gold piece, the famed "Walking Liberty," has multiplied in value 5 times from 1984 to 1991 (provided it was in top condition). Bullion coins, whose value resides solely in the metal they contain, are another story. Like gold bars, they have languished—except for the small, early mintings of the Chinese Panda, which became instant collectibles because they were so cute.

The primary use for platinum and rhodium is in catalytic converters, the devices that reduce pollution in automobile exhaust. For platinum, jewelry runs a close second.

Checkpoints

Risk/Reward—High risk, usually low reward. No interest or dividends.

Liquidity—Depends. Coins are highly liquid. Ingots may have to be assayed before a sale.

Investment Size—From a few hundred dollars (for a small coin) on up.

Attention—Infrequent, unless you own gold stocks. Prices respond to world events.

Goals—Wealth

Duration—Usually indefinite. No timetable with a "just-in-case-the-world-goes-haywire" investment.

Tax—Profits are fully taxable.

8

Gold Bars for Sale

Gross weights of gold bars available for sale:

1 gram
2.5 grams
5 grams
10 grams
1/4 ounce (7.775871 g)
1 tola (11.6638 g)
1/2 ounce (15.5551741)
20 grams
1 ounce (31.1034807 g)
1 tael (37.4175 g)
50 grams
5 tola (58.319 g)
2 ounces (62.206962)
100 grams
10 tola (116.638 g)
5 ounces (155.517404 g)
250 grams
10 ounces (311.034807 g)
500 grams
1 kilogram (1,000 g)
100 ounces (3,110.34807 g)

Source: Credit Suisse

How much gold should you buy?

Most investment advisors recommend investing a maximum of 5% of your assets in gold or other metals. Not only is gold a speculative investment, but it also throws off no interest or dividends (unless you buy mining stocks).

In what form can I buy precious metals?

Bullion: actual bars of metal, called ingots. They need to be stored, and must be assayed (certified for weight and purity) before they can be resold.

Bullion certificates: You get a certificate; the investment company takes care of storage and assaying.

Bullion coins: Issued by countries throughout the world, including the U.S., bullion coins let investors purchase quantities as small as 1/4 ounce, with no need for assaying. Coins still must be safely stored, though.

Mining stocks: Mining stocks pay dividends, unlike the metals themselves. And you don't have to worry about storage.

Options: Options can be purchased for all sorts of metals, as well as for mining stocks.

Futures contracts: A fast and furious way to play. Futures contracts are available for precious, industrial, and strategic metals.

Numismatic coins: Numismatic coins have value beyond their metal, be it historic or esthetic. As with all collectibles, you need to study before you buy. The large quantity of beautiful coins in mediocre condition (condition being a key to value) on the market means the unscrupulous have many opportunities to fleece the unwary.

> *My boy...always try to rub up against money, for if you rub up against money long enough, some of it may rub off on you.*
>
> **Damon Runyon**

Can I buy gold coins for my IRA?

No. Although you can't buy precious metals or numismatic coins for an Individual Retirement Account, you can buy mining stock and U.S. gold and silver coins.

Can I invest in precious metals through a mutual fund?

As of September 1992, 33 mutual funds have traded precious metals. If you invest with a major mutual fund company, its "family" probably includes precious metals funds.

Conventional wisdom says to hold gold in case of bad times. Should I do the same with platinum?

Platinum is an optimist's, not a pessimist's, investment. Since it's a key ingredient in catalytic converters—automobile pollution control devices—the metal's price rises during boom times.

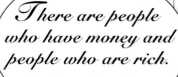

There are people who have money and people who are rich.

Coco Chanel

About Silver...

More than half the silver used in the U.S. goes into photographic film.

The U.S. stopped making silver coins in 1964, substituting copper and nickel when the metal became more valuable than the coins themselves.

In 1980, when the Hunt brothers tried to "corner" the silver market, prices rose as high as $48 an ounce. In 1992, silver cost less than $5 an ounce.

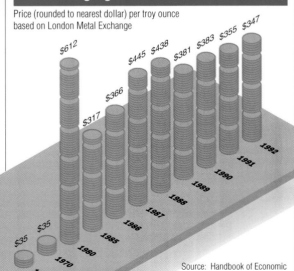

The Changing Price of Gold Since 1960

Price (rounded to nearest dollar) per troy ounce
based on London Metal Exchange

Year	Price
1960	$35
1970	$35
1980	$612
1985	$317
1986	$366
1987	$445
1988	$438
1989	$381
1990	$383
1991	$355
1992	$347

Source: Handbook of Economic Statistics, 1991, CIA

Americans have been allowed to own gold bullion legally only since 1974.

COMMODITIES FUTURES

Traditionally, a **commodity** was defined as a farm product, such as wheat, corn, or pork bellies (used to make bacon), or a mineral, oil, or forest product. Today anything that is traded on the **futures** market—a market in contracts for sales or purchases in the future—is considered a commodity, including stock indexes and T-bills.
● Futures investors use great amounts of leverage, generally paying only 5% to 10% of a contract's actual value to purchase it. In a mercurial marketplace, they can make mountains of money or lose their shirts. Most are simple speculators, just interested in making a profit on the deal, not in the goods they're buying or selling. They can play one of 2 ways: by **going long**—buying a contract to take ownership of a specific product to be delivered on a certain date at a specified price—or by **going short**—contracting to hand over a specific product on a certain date at a specified price. To take profits or cut losses, futures speculators cancel their contract by offsetting it with an equivalent contract for the opposite trade. Be warned—this is an area where amateurs often get badly burned.

DID YOU KNOW?

98% of commodities transactions do not involve delivery of the actual goods.

Who needs futures?

Farmers: as a hedge against fluctuating agricultural prices.

Manufacturing and food-processing corporations: to lock in the price of such raw materials as wheat, corn, pork bellies, orange juice, oil, rubber, etc.

Jewelers: to stabilize the price they pay for gold.

International traders: to lock in values for currencies, stabilizing the costs and profits of future transactions.

Institutional investors: to protect against stock market drops, they may use futures on stock indexes, such as the Standard & Poor's 500-stock index.

Where Commodities Are Traded

Chicago Board Of Trade (CBOT): corn, oats, soybeans, soybean meal, soybean oil, wheat, plywood, gold, silver, commercial paper, GNMA mortgages, Treasury bonds

Chicago Mercantile Exchange (CME): broiler chickens, cattle, eggs, hogs, lumber, pork bellies, potatoes, gold, silver coins, currencies, Treasury bills, certificates of deposit, Eurodollars, S&P 500 Index futures

Coffee, Sugar & Cocoa Exchange (New York City): coffee, sugar, cocoa

Commodity Exchange (New York City): copper, gold, silver, aluminum

Kansas City Board Of Trade: wheat, Value Line stock index futures

Mid America Commodity Exchange (Chicago, IL): corn, oats, soybeans, wheat, gold

Minneapolis Grain Exchange: sunflower seeds, wheat

New York Cotton Exchange: cotton, orange juice, propane

New York Futures Exchange (a subsidiary of the New York Stock Exchange): NYSE composite index, options on futures

New York Mercantile Exchange: imported beef, potatoes, No. 2 heating oil, No. 6 heating oil, gasoline, gold, silver coins, palladium, platinum

There are two times in a man's life when he should not speculate: when he can't afford it, and when he can.

Mark Twain

Checkpoints

Risk/Reward—Very high.

Liquidity—Very high.

Investment Size—From a few hundred dollars—but you'll have to show a high net worth before you open an account with most brokers.

Attention—Constant. Futures prices move in minutes.

Goals—Big gains over short time periods.

Duration—Futures contracts can be held for just days or for many months.

TAX

Tax—All profits are taxable.

9

COLLECTIBLES

If something can be owned, there is probably an individual out there who collects it. The desire to hoard favorite things seems to be a universal human trait, starting with the strings, bottlecaps, or baseball cards you may have saved when you were a child. ● Writ large, the collector's impulse can be channeled into art, antiques, and rare books, à la J.P. Morgan, who assembled the world's great cultural treasures in his New York City home, now a museum. Or it could become an obsession with the works of one person; Thomas Monaghan (founder of Domino's Pizza) has an encyclopedic collection of furnishings by Frank Lloyd Wright. On a more human scale, collecting is not an investment per se—the term "investment" implies an intention to sell as well as buy—but a passionate and intelligent acquisitor may find that his cherished objects gain value once the rest of the world catches up with his taste. ● The thing to remember about collectibles is that it's very difficult to predict if you will make money. Prices for high-quality collectibles, says Robert Salomon, director of research at Salomon Brothers, rise and fall along with the creation and destruction of wealth throughout the world. "The primary appeal of assets like Old Master paintings, Chinese ceramics, or rare stamps," Salomon says, "is that they are a means of proving the financial power of the buyer." On much less grandiose terms, the same could be said for a set of Biedermeier chairs. ● In addition, collectibles, unlike money-market accounts and other traditional investments, will not throw off income, interest, or dividends.

How do you start collecting?

People usually begin collections out of interest in a type of object, such as books, and then subspecialize in an area that captures their imagination and fits their wallets, such as 19th-century nature books. Others may start when they are furnishing a home. What's most important is learning the market, from keeping tabs on prices to understanding the origins and history of the objects you love. Keys to collectibles' value include their **age**, their **quality**, their **rarity**, their **condition**, and how easily you can trace their **origins**.

What makes an object precious?

Age: the term "antique" refers to art and decorative objects at least 100 years old for tax and customs purposes. Cars become antique, qualifying for lower insurance rates, at 25 years old.

Origin: Also called "provenance," this includes information on who owned the object as well as who made it. A strong provenance, possibly including publication in a book or exhibition in a museum, will bolster an object's value. Objects that illuminate social or cultural history may have value for that alone, whether or not they are beautiful.

Quality: Collectors need to be able to gauge workmanship and beauty as well as know the right artists and artisans to buy. Obviously, the better a piece is, the more it will be worth—especially during market slumps. Owners of second-rate Picassos are finding this out in the '90s, to their despair.

Rarity: The more difficult it is to find a piece, the more valuable it may become. For instance, if you have 2 etchings of similar quality by the same artist, but one comes from an edition of 20 and the other from an edition of 2,000, guess which one will be more valuable.

Condition: A piece that has been damaged and repaired almost always loses some of its value. Types of repairs considered acceptable differ dramatically by object. For instance, revarnished wood might not affect the value of an upholstered Victorian chair, but will decimate the value of a Mission oak chair. If, on the other hand, a leg has been broken and reglued, well, never mind.

Checkpoints

Risk/Reward—Low risk, unless you spend big. High rewards are possible, but not worth counting on.

Liquidity—Depends on what you collect. Often low.

Investment Size—From a few dollars to millions.

Attention—Low. May require maintenance/conservation; usually deserves ongoing education.

Goals—Wealth—but mostly pleasure.

Duration—Typically, it is many years.

TAX

Tax—Profits are taxable.

10

95

DID YOU KNOW?

When Renoir's *Au Moulin de la Galette* sold for $78 million in 1990, the Whitney family received 430 times the $165,000 paid for it in 1929. That's an annual rate of return of just 10%, achieved much more frequently among stock market investors than among art collectors.

It is preoccupation with possession, more than anything else, that prevents men from living freely and nobly.

Bertrand Russell

BUYING AT AUCTION

Auctions are the ultimate meeting of buyer and seller, a microcosm of the marketplace, a pure form of competition. They are exciting, fun and occasionally a source of bargains.

What should I know about buying at an auction?

• **Know what you're looking at, or find someone who does.** Auctioned goods are sold as is, so inspect objects carefully. If you don't notice a crack in a vase until after you've bought it, you're stuck. Although better auction houses report items' condition in their catalogues, high-ticket collectors often ask a trusted professional, such as a favorite dealer, to check out a few pieces at the preview.

• **Set a price limit and stick to it.** Everyone is susceptible to auction fever, but no one likes to feel he overpaid once temperatures are back to normal. This goes for backyard furniture as well as fine art and jewelry. The best protection is to set a price limit before bidding begins—one that accounts for the auction house's 10% buyer's premium.

• **Learn auction house catch phrases.** Catalogues have their own language; those who know it come to a sale well briefed on the value of items on the block. "Attributed to" Rembrandt does not mean there's proof the Dutch master laid a hand on the piece, but it's stronger than "in the style of" or "school of" Rembrandt. "After" Rembrandt is weaker still. If you're dealing with a reputable auction house, you can count on solid connoisseurship to back up the description.

• **Read the fine print.** Auction catalogues have terms of sale, and they are worth knowing before you bid. The terms of sale will list the buyer's premium—usually 10%, paid to the auction house—as well as what forms of payment are acceptable. A few auctioneers guarantee the authenticity and condition of items they sell; you'll find out by reading the catalogue. (Most adhere strictly to the principle of *caveat emptor*.)

HIRING AN APPRAISER

Before you donate Aunt Bessie's silver service to your church rummage sale, it might be wise to find out what it's really worth—or at least, whether it's actually worthless. To do so, hire an appraiser, an expert professional who specializes in evaluating the type of objects you own.

How do I find an appraiser?

Finding an appraiser is not difficult, but finding a good one may be. Art and antique dealers often appraise items, but if they're also potential buyers, they face a conflict of interest. Many auction houses hold periodic appraisal days, when anyone can bring in their belongings for a valuation. The Appraisers Association of America publishes a national directory of its members, who must have a minimum of 3 years' experience. Certified members must pass a written exam.

SOURCES

Maine Antique Digest
P.O. Box 645
Waldoboro, ME 04572
207-832-7534

This monthly publication features articles on antiques of all types, plus auction reviews.

To order a directory of the members of the Appraisers Associaltion of America, send $12.95 to Appraisers Association of America, 60 E. 42nd St., New York, NY 10165

FURTHERMORE

Collectibles for the '90s

animation art: "cels," the celluloid paintings used to make cartoons, are now major auction house draws. In 1990, Steven Spielberg paid an astonishing $121,000 to purchase a 1937 Mickey Mouse cel at Sotheby's.

antiques: from flea market finds to million dollar masterpieces, antiques offer beauty, history, and a place to sit.

art: while fine arts prices languish, those wealthy collectors who haven't gone bankrupt (or to jail) are buying high-quality modern and Old Master works at prices as much as 30% below their late-1980s highs.

baseball cards and memorabilia: pre-1950 baseball cards (more modern ones are not rare enough), though expensive now, have potential for long-term appreciation.

cars: although Ferrari prices dropped after the 1987 stock market crash (Ferraris were a favorite "toy" on Wall Street), other collectible cars, ranging from 1960s Mustangs to elegant 1920s Bugattis, are going strong. New cars costing more than $30,000 are subject to the recent 10% luxury tax, but not used ones, whether you've found a vintage Mercedes gullwing or last year's model. Watch out, though: You may have to install safety devices like seatbelts and headrests if you actually plan to drive a car built before the mid-1960s.

clocks and watches: check out your grandfather's gold watch: It may be worth much, much more than you think. Whereas clocks have been collected for as long as they've existed, interest in watches just started heating up in the past decade.

Depression glass: a flea market favorite. Pretty, plentiful, and relatively cheap, Depression glass looks great on the table and appreciates steadily. One caveat: Contemporary reissues and imitations are plentiful now, so make sure you're getting what you've paid for.

jewelry: unlike contemporary gems, antique jewelry is not subject to the new 10% luxury tax on jewelry worth more than $10,000.

rugs: beautiful and functional, Middle Eastern and Oriental rugs have been collected for centuries. Contemporary passions rage for American Indian rugs and weavings.

silver: although the value of the metal itself is languishing, silver objects of all kinds, from Georgian silver to French deco, are being heavily collected.

toys: a form of folk art, 19th-century toys are important collectibles now. And 20th-century toys are coming into their own: a 1934 Monopoly game (a rare, pre-Parker Brothers edition) was auctioned for $4,400 in 1991.

10

LIMITED PARTNERSHIPS

What's "limited" about limited partnerships? In the '90s, practically everything. The tax-law changes of 1986 have made it almost impossible for investors to deduct the paper losses these vehicles were generally designed to generate (that is, until the investment eventually paid off); today, you can deduct partnership losses only from investment income, not from earned income, taking almost all the shelter out of tax shelters. Add to that the real estate slump, which slashed the value of the most popular types of partnerships, and the limited ability to sell many partnerships on the open market, and you have all the ingredients you need to cook up a terrible slump. ● If, however, you get most of your income from investments, and are willing to do your own research on the viability of partnerships, you can do well. Today, many partnership shares are selling for as little as 20% to 35% of their original issue price, making this a true buyer's market.

SOURCES

Chicago Partnership Board
800-272-6273

Equity Resources Group
617-876-4000

EquityLine Properties
800-327-9990

Liquidity Fund
800-548-7355

MacKenzie Securities
800-854-8357

National Partnership Exchange
800-356-2739

Partnership Securities Exchange
415-763-5555

Raymond James & Associates
800-441-4103

If you want to buy or sell partnership shares, call several of these sources; because the market is so thin, prices can vary greatly.

How do limited partnerships work?

Limited partnerships sell interests to individuals who do not take an active role in managing the investment. That job falls to the **general partner**, who selects the investment, acquires it, and provides the necessary paperwork to the limited partners. Classical limited partnerships were designed to show tax losses at their inception, yet were meant to yield a profit when the investment matured and its assets were sold off several years down the line. Because of their tax advantages, limited partnerships were an ideal way to fund large-scale, high-risk projects with payoffs far in the future, such as oil wells, office buildings, and movie deals.

In the real estate area, some limited partnerships were designed to be less risky, as well as less tax-deductible, in order to generate a steady income stream. These partnerships eschewed debt, buying buildings for cash, and making regular income distributions to the partners. Although tax reform didn't kill these partnerships, the real estate slump has done a good job of slenderizing their bottom lines.

What's a master limited partnership?

A master limited partnership is traded on the stock market rather than being sold privately, giving it the liquidity of a common stock. At the same time, it enjoys the tax benefits of limited partnerships: Profits are not taxed until they are distributed to the shareholders. With common stocks, on the other hand, profits are taxed twice, once as corporate income, and again as shareholders' personal income when they are distributed as dividends.

FURTHERMORE

Popular Partnerships

Real estate—offices, shopping centers, apartments, even nursing homes

Oil and Gas

Equipment leasing—including computers, jet planes, cable television systems

Movie and theater productions

Checkpoints

HIGH
LOW

Risk/Reward—Since most limited partnerships are no longer tax shelters, the rewards have become low and the risks remain high.

HIGH
LOW

Liquidity—Very low, except for master limited partnerships sold on the stock exchanges.

LARGE
SMALL

Investment Size—Usually several thousand dollars.

STAY ALERT
RELAX & ENJOY

Attention—Moderate.

WEALTH   RETIREMENT

Goals—Wealth, possibly retirement; over the long term, partnerships may come out of their slump and pay off big.

DAYS   MONTHS   YEARS

Duration—Years. A long-term investment, pure and simple.

TAX

Tax—Some partnerships' losses can be written off against other investment income.

11

99

ESTATE PLANNING

It's hard to believe how few Americans pay attention to estate planning: Some 75% of us die intestate (without a will). Not only do three-fourths of us leave the disposition of our assets to the faceless bureaucrats of whatever state we live in, but we also allow them to decide who will raise our children, what funds they can use, and to what standards they will be held. Now is that sensible?

> *When you have told anyone you have left him a legacy, the only decent thing to do is to die at once.*
>
> **Samuel Butler**

● Maybe people figure that they don't need a will because they are worth less than $600,000, the amount at which estates become subject to punishing federal taxes, or because they are leaving everything to their spouses, making the entire estate tax-exempt (until the spouses leave it to someone, that is). Maybe they believe that they will never die. None of these rationalizations is valid.

Do I need a lawyer to write a will?

No, but you probably should consult one. Although in most states, **holographic** (handwritten) wills are not legally valid, typed and witnessed wills—preferably notarized—are just fine. A good business stationery store will carry boilerplate forms for wills, and a careful person can fill one out himself. Laws governing wills are many and complex, however, and it can't hurt to have an attorney go over the finished product, especially when there are children.

Who needs to know about my will?

For one, the people who are to carry out your instructions when your will take effect. The **executor**, or person who executes the disposition of property, should know what you're asking him to do, feel confident about doing it, and know where the will is. The same is true for your spouse, probably the prime beneficiary of your will, if not the executor as well. (If your spouse is the executor, be sure to name an alternate, for obvious reasons.) The **guardian** you name for minor children should also be aware of your will, and should promise to let you know if for any reason he no longer feels prepared to take on that responsibility. If you put assets in a trust, the **trustee** should also be aware of his role in your affairs.

What is probate?

Probate is when a court reviews and approves a will, a nitpicky, expensive process that generally takes as long as a year. This is what drives executors crazy. Property must be evaluated and its ownership established. A lot of forms get filled out. And in the end, there may be taxes as well as fees. The better the order in which you keep your affairs, the less hassle for your heirs.

S O U R C E S

American Bar Association
750 North Lake Shore Dr.
Chicago, IL 60611-4497
312-988-5000

Publishes pamphlet, Planning for Life and Death, *a general introduction to how the disposition of property, tax liabilities, and personal needs can be protected by a will.*

S O U R C E S

Concern for Dying/ Society for the Right to Die
250 W 57th St.
New York, NY 10107

Can provide forms to write a living will.

THE NUMBERS

Median Net Worth for Americans 65 and Older

Annual Household Income	Median Net Worth Age 65 and Older
$20,400–$ 30,799	$141,811
$30,800–$ 46,599	$201,562
$46,600 and up	$343,015
$75,000 and up*	$500,000–$700,000
All households (Median income: $ 23,796)	$73,471

Source: U.S. Census Bureau
* Source: Money Magazine

FURTHERMORE

Do It Yourself— Estate Planning Software

Personal Financial Planning Set
Heiler Software ($96)
800-888-7667

Includes asset management, insurance analysis, education financing, cash flow, estate analysis.

Trust Maker
Legisoft Inc.
415-566-9136

This program guides you through the process of setting up a living trust.

12

Life is short. The sooner that a man begins to enjoy his wealth the better.

Samuel Johnson

What's the difference between a will, a living will, and a living trust?

A living will tells doctors how to care for you if you become incapacitated and cannot speak for yourself. It has nothing to do with your regular will. A living trust, also called an inter vivos trust, is a corporation you set up to own and manage your property while you are alive, and to distribute your assets to heirs when you are not. It is an extremely flexible type of trust that's often used by wealthy people and frequent travelers as a way to minimize probate and estate-tax hassles, as well as to keep their finances out of the public eye. (Wills, because they are probated in court, become a matter of public record.) Living trusts are, however, expensive to set up. A lawyer must establish the trust, and then property must be legally transferred to it. A trustee must be named to manage the trust; if you name a trustee other than yourself, that person must be paid, and fees for qualified trustees, such as banks, attorneys, and money managers, are high.

Why do people need trusts?

One reason is to keep assets private. Another is to minimize estate taxes. If a person has a large estate, for instance, he can leave $600,000 to his spouse—keeping her assets within the amount exempt from estate taxes—and put the rest in a testamentary trust (a trust established in a will) that gives the spouse income during her lifetime, then places the property itself in the hands of other heirs, such as children.

Another reason to place assets in trust is to protect the rights of children when there has been more than one marriage. A spouse has a legal right to contest assets willed completely to children from an earlier marriage, even when the spouse has money of his own. He may not have the right to contest a trust. Of course, a well-written prenuptial agreement can protect children just as well.

What are the most common types of trusts?

Charitable remainder trust: A trust that invests the principal and provides income for specific beneficiaries, such as a spouse; but when the trust is dissolved, the assets remaining in it are donated to charity. Every time an individual adds principal to such a trust, he can take a tax deduction for a charitable donation.

Grantor retained income trust (GRIT): A trust that may provide income for its founder, but whose principal belongs to the founder's heirs. Assets donated to such a trust can grow tax-free, but the GRIT can last no longer than 10 years.

Insurance trust: A trust funded by a life-insurance policy. Often, insurance trusts are used by parents of young children; they may also be used to cover estate-tax liabilities, especially if most of the estate is in property, such as real estate or art, that heirs won't want to cash in for the tax man.

Qualified terminable interest property trust (QTIP): A trust that provides income and, perhaps, some assets to support a surviving spouse, but that passes on the remaining assets to others, such as children, after the spouse's death.

Testamentary trust: A trust that's established in a person's will.

SOURCES

American Association of Retired Persons
1909 K St., NW
Washington, D.C. 20049
202-434-2277

Can provide information on estate laws and taxes in all 50 states; plus instructions for writing a durable power of attorney, authorizing a spouse, relative, or friend to act in your name if you are incapacitated.

What American Families Own

	1951	1971	1991
Answering machine	0	0	42%
Cable TV service	0	7%	53%
Car	60%	83%	87%
More than one car	4%	35%	53%
Nintendo	0	0	32%
Personal computer	0	0	26%
Television	23%	94%	98%
More than one television	0	28%	71%
Telephone service	62%	91%	93%
VCR	0	0	79%
More than one VCR	0	0	28%
Video camera/camcorder	0	0	18%

Investments at a Glance

Investment Type	Page	Minimum $	Potential for Capital Growth	Income
Piggy bank	10	1 cent	Very low to none	Very low to none
Checking account	59	$100	Very low to none	Very low or none to limited
Savings account	59	$100	Very low to none	Limited to moderate
Certificate of deposit	61	$250	Very low[2]	Moderate
Series EE savings bonds	36	$25	Very low to none	Moderate
Mutual funds	46	$100–$2,000	Very low or none to very high[4]	Very low or none to very high[4]
U.S. Treasury notes	38	$5,000	Moderate[2,5]	Moderate
U.S. Treasury bonds	38	$1,000	Moderate[5]	Moderate to somewhat high
Ginnie Mae, Sallie Mae, or Fannie Mae	37	$10,000–$25,000	Moderate[5]	Moderate to somewhat high
Corporate bonds	37	$10,000–$25,000[7]	Very low or none to very high[5]	Moderate to very high
Municipal bonds	45	$10,000–$25,000[7]	Moderate to very high[5]	Moderate to somewhat high
Stocks	16	$1,000–$30,000[7]	Moderate to very high	Very low or none to moderate
Limited partnerships	98	$100,000[10]	Very low or none to very high	Very low or none to very high
Precious metals	88	$350–$50,000	Limited to very high	None
Options	84	$50,000[10]	Very high	Very low to none[11]
Futures Commodities	92	$100,000[10]	Very high	None

Legend:

[1] Inflation may diminish the value of this investment over time.

[2] If investment is "rolled over" when it matures, it will compound, yielding a small amount of capital growth.

[3] Money is accessible if you are willing to pay a penalty.

[4] Position in range depends on type of mutual fund (see chart, pp. 48–49).

[5] Long-term bonds gain value on the open market when interest rates fall.

[6] Long-term bonds lose value on the open market when interest rates rise.

[7] Although you can get into stocks for less than $100, quality stocks generally require a mininum investment of $1,000. Higher number is investment required to acquire a well-diversified portfolio.

[8] High-yielding "junk" bonds run a high risk of default.

[9] Ideally, stock investors should commit their money for at least 5 years or so.

[10] Although actual investment is not so high, a minimum net worth generally is necessary.

[11] Selling options against stocks that you own can produce income.

Risk	Liquidity	Time Horizon	Attention Required	Tax Status
Limited[1]	Very high	Short	Very low to none	No taxes
Limited[1]	Very high	Short	Limited	Interest is taxable
Limited[1]	Very high	Short to long	Very low to none	Interest is taxable
Moderate[1]	Limited[3]	Short to intermediate	Limited	Interest is taxable
Limited[1]	Limited	Short to long	Very low to none	Interest exempt from state and local taxes
Very low or none to somewhat high[4]	Very high	Long	Limited to somewhat high[3]	Depends on type of fund (see chart, pp. 48–49)
Moderate[1]	Somewhat high	Intermediate	Limited to moderate	Interest exempt from state and local taxes
Limited to somewhat high[1,6]	Very high	Long	Moderate	Interest exempt from state and local taxes
Moderate[1,6]	Somewhat high to very high	Long	Moderate	Taxable
Moderate to very high[1,6,8]	None or somewhat high to very high	Long	Moderate to very high	Taxable
Moderate to very high[1,6,8]	None or somewhat high to very high	Long	Moderate to very high	Income free of federal, and possibly state and local taxes. Capital gains taxable
Moderate to very high	Very high	Long[9]	Moderate to very high	Taxable
Moderate to very high	Very low or none to moderate	Long	Moderate to very high	Check with accountant
Moderate to very high	Moderate to very high	Short to long	Very low or none to somewhat high	Taxable
Very high	Very high	Short	Very high	Taxable
Very high	Very high	Short	Very high	Taxable

GLOSSARY

12b-1 fee: a charge investors pay annually to cover the fund's marketing and advertising expenses. p. 50

401(k): if your employer offers one, you can save up to $8,475 a year of pretax dollars—often matched by the company with additional funds—which will grow, tax-deferred, until you retire. p. 73

adjustable-rate mortgage (ARM): a mortgage whose interest rate shifts, usually twice a year, to reflect general changes in interest rates. p. 79

Alternative Minimum Tax: a special income tax for high earners with tax-exempt investments. pp. 39 & 42

American Depositary Receipts (ADRs): certificates of ownership of foreign stocks that are held by American banks. pp.19 & 35

AMEX: the American Stock Exchange. p. 19

amortization: paying off the principal (the actual amount lent) of a loan. pp. 79 & 80

asked price: the investor's buying price. p. 33

at par: when a bond sells for its face value, typically $1,000. p.41

average maturity: the average of the maturities of bonds or other fixed-income instruments in a bond or money-market fund portfolio. p. 45

back-end load: a commission paid when you sell your shares instead of when you buy. Often these loads, also known as **contingent deferred sales charges** or **redemption fees**, disappear after you've owned your shares 5 to 10 years. p. 50

bad banks: banks that have become insolvent. p. 62

balloon payment: a lump sum of principal due at the end of a mortgage term. p. 79

basis point: one hundredth of 1% (0.01%). Used when discussing bond yields. p. 45

bearer bond: a bond certificate, held by the bond owner (or broker), with coupons that are detached and presented to collect interest. p. 45

beta coefficient (beta): a number that compares the risk of an investment with the risk of the overall stock market. p. 52

bid price: the investor's selling price. p. 33

blue chip: a truly stellar stock, with magnificent prospects for long-term growth, a longstanding reputation for paying its dividends. p. 31

bond: a certificate stating that someone owes you money. When you buy a bond, you buy a debt: You become a lender. p.36

book value per share: the current **net worth** of a company (that is, the value of its **assets** minus its **liabilities**) divided by the number of shares on the market. If a stock's price is lower than its book value, and there's no looming business disaster depressing its prices, it's a bargain. p. 20

bullion: gold or silver sold in bars, called **ingots**. They need to be stored, and must be **assayed** (certified for weight and purity) before they can be resold. p. 90

bullion coins: coins whose value resides solely in the precious metal they contain. p. 90

call date: provision in most bonds entitling issuers to buy out their debt before it matures so they can refinance at a lower interest rate. pp. 43 & 45

call: an option for the right to buy. pp. 84 & 87

cap: a limit on how much adjust-able-rate mortgage payments can change. The cap can limit interest charged, or the dollar amount of the mortgage payment. p. 79

capital gains: profits from the rising price of investments. p. 56

closed-end funds: mutual funds that issue limited numbers of shares, which are traded on the stock market as if they were common stocks. p. 47

commercial banks: banks that originally lent to businesses, as well as issuing checking accounts, savings accounts, and credit cards to consumers. Commercial bank deposits are insured by the Federal Deposit Insurance Corporation (FDIC). p. 60

commodity: traditionally, a farm, mineral, oil, or forest product. Today, anything that is traded on the **futures** market is considered a commodity, including stock indexes and T-bills. p. 92

credit union: a consumer-owned cooperative that lends to its members rather than the public at large. Traditionally, credit unions are founded by labor unions or large corporations and are open only to members or employees. p. 60

current yield: the rate of interest based on the current price of a bond. You can figure it out yourself by comparing the dollar payment you receive with the bond's purchase price. Also, the yield of a stock's dividends as a percentage of its current share price. p. 45

debt/equity ratio: compares what a company owes to what it owns, by dividing its debt by its net worth. p. 22

discount: a price lower than the face value of an investment. p. 41

dividends: the direct payments corporations send to each **stockholder**. p. 17

Dow Jones Industrial Average (DJIA): an index of 30 giant-corporation stocks representing major industrial sectors of the economy. Even though the DJIA (also called the Dow) activity may not always reflect the rest of the market—nor the economy as a whole—it's typically the number you hear reported on the business news. p. 23

equity: ownership. When you buy a house, you have the equity represented by the down payment, and the bank, or mortgage owner, has the rest. As you pay off your mortgage, your equity increases. p. 79

family of funds: mutual fund companies with a variety of funds under their roofs market themselves as fund "families." They allow for ease of switching investments from one type to another, and may have combined monthly statements and other amenities. p. 52

fixed-rate mortgage: a mortgage with a single rate of interest for its entire term. p. 79

FNMA bonds: "Fannie Maes," issued by the Federal National Mortgage Association, contain federally sponsored (not guaranteed) mortgages and are issued in $10,000 denominations. p. 38

futures: contracts for sales or purchases in the future. Futures investors use great amounts of leverage, generally paying only 5% to 10% of a contract's actual value to purchase it. pp. 92 & 93

general partner: manager of a limited partnership, responsible for selecting the investment, acquiring it, and providing the necessary paperwork to the limited partners. p. 99

GNMA bonds: "Ginnie Maes" are issued by a corporation within the federal Department of Housing and Urban Development (HUD), which guarantees pools of home mortgages. Sold in $25,000 denominations, Ginnie Maes have 25-year terms, but usually last about 12 years. They are not exempt from any form of income tax. pp. 38 & 48

going public: beginning to sell shares to the general public. p. 22

growth stock: one whose value is expected to grow dramatically over time. Its return comes primarily from its rising share price, and not from dividends. p. 30

Individual Retirement Account (IRA): a special account in which your money can grow, tax-deferred, until you withdraw it age 59$\frac{1}{2}$. pp. 67 & 68

ingot: bar of gold, silver, or other precious metal. p. 90

Initial Public Offerings (IPOs): first-time sales of stock to the general public. p. 19

intermediate-term bond: a bond that matures in 2 to 10 years. p. 000

Keogh plan: with a Keogh, a self-employed investor can set aside 25% of his earned income up to a ceiling of $30,000. pp. 67 & 70

leverage: borrowing. Leverage allows you to make a large trans-action with a small amount of money, maximizing profits, but at high risks. p. 85

leveraged buyout (LBO): when private investors buy a company by putting up corporate assets to back vast quantities of junk bonds. p. 37

limited partnerships: partnerships that sell interests to individuals who do not take an active role in managing the invest-ment. Recent changes in the tax laws have reduced the appeal of limited partnerships. p. 98

long-term bond: a bond that matures in more than 10 years. p. 40

low-load funds: funds that charge low sales commissions, usually about 3%. p. 50

margin account: an account where you trade with money bor-rowed from your brokerage. p. 85

master limited partnership: a limited partnership that is traded on the stock market rather than being sold privately. p. 99

Moody's Investor Services: a corporation that rates bond issuers' creditworthiness. pp. 40 & 43

municipal bonds: states, cities, and their agencies sell bonds to raise money for roads and bridges, sewers, industrial development, college dorms, even environmental preservation, and to finance their cash needs. These bonds are exempt from federal income tax. p. 49

mutual funds: investment companies that pool money from thousands of individuals and invest it all as a lump sum. They may buy vast portfolios of stocks, bonds, gold, foreign currency, options, or several of the latter in combination. They range in philosophy and method from the super-conservative to the ultra-daring. pp. 46 & 49

NASDAQ: the National Association of Securities Dealers Automated Quotations, the computerized trading system for over-the-counter stocks (those not traded at a stock exchange). p. 19

net asset value (NAV) per share: the value of all the investments owned by a mutual fund, divided by its number of shares. p. 47

no-load funds: funds that don't charge a sales commission. p. 50

numismatic coins: coins that have collectible as well as bullion value. p. 90

NYSE: the New York Stock Exchange. pp. 19 & 24

open-end funds: mutual funds that issue unlimited numbers of shares, which are sold to—or bought from—the public directly. p. 47

option: the contractual *right* either to buy or to sell something. p. 84

over-the-counter stocks: stocks of corporations that, though publicly traded, are too small to qualify for an exchange listing. They are sold instead through a computer-linked network of suppliers, called **market makers**, and brokers. p. 32

point: one percent of a loan amount. Most banks charge a 2 to 3 point fee to finalize a mortgage. p. 79

portfolio manager: the individual who makes investment decisions for a mutual fund. p. 51

preferred stock: shares that have "first dibs" on a company's profits for dividend payments, but may lack voting rights. Corporations, which don't pay taxes on dividends, are the most frequent buyers of preferred stock. p. 29

premium: a price higher than the face value of an investment. p. 41

prepayment penalty: a charge levied when you pay extra on your mortgage before it's due. Today, few lenders charge a prepayment penalty. p. 79

price/earnings ratio (p/e): also called a **multiple**. The price of a stock divided by the amount of money it earns per share (listed in its **annual report**). For instance, if a stock's price is $25, and it earned $2.50 last year, its p/e would be 10. p. 20

price-to-book ratio: compares the company's share price with its **book value** (the company's total assets minus its liabilities) per share. See **book value per share.** p. 20

principal: the actual money lent, as opposed to the interest. p. 79

prospectus: a document that is legally required to cover an investment's history, activities, expenses, and future plans in detail. p. 55

put: an option for the right to sell. pp. 84 & 87

real return: gains after inflation has been counted out. p. 31

redemption fee: a commission paid when an investor *sells* his shares. p. 50

registered bonds: bonds that exist only in electronic form. Interest is automatically credited to your brokerage or bank account, instead of being paid in check form upon receipt of your bond coupons. pp. 40 & 45

REIT: Real Estate Investment Trust. p. 82

RELP: Real Estate Limited Partnership. pp. 82 & 99

return on equity (ROE): a stock's ROE is found by dividing the corporation's net income by its capital (the value of its stock plus earnings not distributed to share-holders, or **retained earnings**).p. 22

sales load: a commission. Mutual fund loads range from 0%–8%; those funds that charge the highest commissions typically are available only from brokers.p. 50

savings & loan institutions: those lucky S&Ls that survived the real-estate collapse of the late '80s and early '90s still lend to individuals and corporations who want to buy houses and other real estate. S&L deposits, once insured by the Federal Savings and Loan Insurance Corporation (FSLIC), are now covered by the FDIC or state agencies for bank insurance. p. 60

self-amortizing: loan payments that include both interest and principal, so the loan wipes itself out at the end of its term. p. 80

selling short: selling stock the investor does not own. A short-seller believes that the stock's price will fall, and that he will be able to buy it later, or **cover his short position,** for less money than he made when he sold the stock. p. 26

share: an individual unit of stock. p. 17

short-term bond: a bond that usually matures in less than 2 years. p. 40

SLMA Bonds: "Sallie Maes" work like Ginnie Maes and Fannie Maes, except that they are issued by the federal Student Loan Management Agency, and are backed by pools of student loans. Like Ginnie Maes, they are 100% federally guaranteed. p. 38

spread: the difference between the bid (selling) price and the asked (buying) price. pp. 33 & 45

Standard & Poor's: a company that measures the financial soundness of public and private corporations, rating bonds, tracking stock performance, and creating its own indexes to track the performance of the stock market as a whole. p. 33

Standard & Poor's 500 (S&P 500): an index of 500 stocks chosen to make up a microcosm of the entire stock market. The S&P 500 is often used as a benchmark for assessing investment performance. p. 19

stock: units of ownership of a corporation. p. 17

stockbrokers: salespeople licensed to carry out trades on one or more stock exchanges. Two basic types of brokers, **full-service** and **discount,** can both sell and buy stocks, as well as bonds, mutual funds, and other financial instruments. pp. 19 & 23

strike price: the price per share at which you can exercise an option. p. 85

tax-deferred annuities (TDAs): contracts that allow an investment company (typically an insurance firm) to invest your money and dole it back to you after you retire. You will need after-tax dollars to buy a TDA, but, as with an IRA, the money in the annuity will grow tax-free until it is withdrawn. p. 67

total return: a performance report that tracks an investment's yield and gains or losses in its asset value. p. 44

Treasury bills: better known as **T-bills,** their terms go from 3 to 12 months. Bills are bought at a discount from their face value of $10,000. The difference between the purchase price and the $10,000 bill holders receive when the bill matures constitutes the interest. p. 43

Treasury bonds: the longest-term debt, bonds can have maturities of as much as 30 years. They pay interest every 6 months and are issued in $1,000 denominations. p. 38

Treasury notes: terms run from 2 to 10 years. Notes pay interest every 6 months. Notes with terms of less than 5 years have a par value of $5,000; those with terms of 5 years or more have a par value of $1,000. p. 38

triple tax-free: interest exempt from federal, state, and local income taxes. p. 49

unit trust: a bond-investment pool that buys a portfolio and holds it until the trust matures, only rein-vesting dividends and proceeds from bonds that are called. When the trust's shares are sold out, it closes to new investors. p. 44

vested: eligible for pension ben-efits even if you leave the company. p. 75

yield to maturity: a yield calcu-lation that factors in the gain or loss you face when your bond matures or is redeemed. p. 41

yield: the amount of income an investment provides. p. 50